·303-INCH MACHINE GUNS AND SMALL ARMS.

40 / W.O. / 3288

NOMENCLATURE OF PARTS, STRIPPING, ASSEMBLING, ACTION, JAMS, MISSFIRES, FAILURES, AND INSPECTION OF:

- (1.) Rifles, Short, **M.L.E.**
- (2.) ,, Charger Loading **M.L.E.**
- (3.) ,, Magazine, ·303-inch, pattern 1914.
- (4.) Pistols, Webley.
- (5.) Gun, Maxim, ·303-inch.
- (6.) ,, Vickers, ·303-inch.
- (7.) ,, Lewis, ·303-inch.
- (8.) ,, Hotchkiss, ·303-inch.

ORDNANCE COLLEGE. (REVISED EDITION—1917.)

The Naval & Military Press Ltd

Published by

The Naval & Military Press Ltd
Unit 5 Riverside, Brambleside
Bellbrook Industrial Estate
Uckfield, East Sussex
TN22 1QQ England

Tel: +44 (0)1825 749494

www.naval-military-press.com
www.nmarchive.com

The Library & Archives Department at the Royal Armouries Museum, Leeds, specialises in the history and development of armour and weapons from earliest times to the present day. Material relating to the development of artillery and modern fortifications is held at the Royal Armouries Museum, Fort Nelson.

For further information contact:
Royal Armouries Museum, Library, Armouries Drive, Leeds, West Yorkshire LS10 1LT

Or visit the Museum's website at
www.armouries.org.uk

In reprinting in facsimile from the original, any imperfections are inevitably reproduced and the quality may fall short of modern type and cartographic standards.

MAGAZINE RIFLES IN THE SERVICE.

Long Rifles.

Magazine Lee-Metford (M.L.M.) Mark I Issued 1889.
    ,,   ,,   ,,   ,,   ,, I*   ,,   1892.
    ,,   ,,   ,,   ,,   ,, II   ,,   1894.
    ,,   ,,   ,,   ,,   ,, II*   ,,   1895.
    ,,   ,, Enfield (M.L.E.) ,, I   ,,   1896.
    ,,   ,,   ,,   ,,   ,, I*   ,,   1899.

These rifles will now be found chiefly in the R.N. and Colonial Forces. The Metford system of rifling permitted excessive wear of the barrel when cordite was used as the propellent, so the Enfield system with fewer and deeper grooves was introduced. As the Metford barrels wear out, they are replaced by Enfield barrels.

A large number of M.L.M., Mark II* and M.L.E. rifles have been converted to charger-loading; the Mark I retains the L.E. sights, Mark I* is fitted with an improved back-sight, both are known as M.L.E. charger-loading rifles and are issued to the Territorial Force. Many of the later patterns of Long Rifles have been converted to Short Rifles, known as converted Mark II, II*, and IV.

Rifle, Charger-Loading, Magazine Lee-Enfield, Mark I and I*.

Converted from M.L.M., Mark II*, and M.L.E., Mark I and I*, for the use of the Territorial Force.

Mark I first issued in 1914, sighted for Mark VII ammunition.
Mark I* issued 1908, resighted for Mark VII ammunition, 1914.

Short Rifles.

Rifle, short, Magazine Lee-Enfield, Mark I, issued 1904.
    ,,   ,,   ,,   ,,   ,,   ,, I*   ,,   1907.
    ,,   ,,   ,,   ,,   ,,   ,, I***   ,,   1914.†
    ,,   ,,   ,,   ,,   ,,   ,, III   ,,   1907.
    ,,   ,,   ,,   ,,   ,,   ,, III*   ,,   1916.

In addition to the above, the later patterns of the Long Rifle have been converted to Short Rifles, as follows:—

R.S.M.L.E. converted Mark II, conforming to S.R. Mark I.
    ,,   ,,   ,, II*   ,,   ,,   ,, I*.
    ,,   ,,   ,, IV   ,,   ,,   ,, III.

The converted rifles conform to the new rifles of the same date, except for a few components taken from the old rifle and utilised in the conversion instead of manufacturing new components to the pattern adopted in Short Rifles.

---

† Converted from Mark I*.

The "Short Rifle" was introduced in 1904 to replace the "Long Rifle" and the "Carbine." It is issued to all branches of the Service, and the following are the chief points of difference between it and the Long Rifle:—

1. Average Marks I, I*, I*** II, and II* about 1 lb. lighter, Marks III, III* and IV about 8 ozs. lighter.
2. Barrel smaller in diameter and 5 inches shorter.
3. Improved sighting arrangements.
4. Adapted for charger loading.
5. Trigger has a double pull-off.
6. Barrel completely covered by handguards and stock. Great attention is paid to the correct adjustment of the stock fore-end and of the nose-cap. The barrel is connected to the stock by the inner band and spring, with ·002" clearance between barrel and band. The opening in the nose-cap for the barrel is elliptical, with a spring stud to press the barrel against the top of the opening. Clearance ·002". The function of the spring stud is to retain the barrel in an unvarying position with reference to the nose-cap.

7. All rifles that have been converted and resighted for Mark VII ammunition are marked II.V. on the barrel: C.L. Rifles in front and Short Rifles behind the back-sight.

Rifle, Magazine, ·303-*inch Pattern* 1914.

Weight about 9 lbs. 6 ozs.
Length 3 ft. 10¼-ins.
Magazine holds 5 cartridges.
M.V. 2,380 f.s.

Main features.—Strength and simplicity, fewer and lighter components, heavier and stronger barrel, simpler form of stocking up, lighter nose-cap, improved balance, and no loose butts.

Increased sight radius combined with a battle sight. Bolt locking gives greater rigidity, magazine entirely in stock, more reliable feed, and when empty, platform fouls the bolt.

Fewer projections facilitate handling.

Directions for Stripping Rifles, Short, Magazine Lee-Enfield, Marks I, I*, I*** and III, III*. Also Converted Short Rifles, Marks II, II* and IV, and C.L. Rifles.

Tools.—None but the authorised tools should be used, and then only for the purpose for which intended, *e.g.*, a small screwdriver should not be used to remove or replace large screws, nor should a large screwdriver be used for small screws, &c. The tools should be laid out on the bench to the right of the vice, close to the flower, and the component parts of the rifle, as stripped, on the left side of vice. This arrangement prevents the tools and parts of rifle from becoming mixed.

The following is a list of the tools which are supplied for use when stripping and assembling rifles:—

Designation of Tool.	No.	Use of Tool.
Anvil, stock butt, M.L.E.R.S. (Short rifles).	1	For attaching stock butts that have slightly swelled.
Anvil, stock butt, M.R. (R.O.L.).	1	
Braces, armourers	1	For use with the various bits.
Bits, screwdriver :—		
Butt plate screw	1	For removing or replacing screws butt plate.
Stock bolt	1	For removing, replacing, or tightening stock bolt.
Centre punch	1	For fixing fore-sight, also for centre-punching certain screws.
Clams, armourers, standing vice.	1	Cork or buff lined for use with the vice when gripping the rifle to prevent damage to the woodwork, &c.
Corks, clam	2	To prevent damage to fittings.
Drifts, fore-end M.L.M.R. Mark II.	1	For removal and replacement of the stock fore-end.
Drifts, pin, fixing, washer, pin axis sight back.	1	For removing and replacing the pin fixing.
Drifts, sight axis pin, M.L.M.	1	For removing axis pins.
Drifts, magazine catch-pin, M.L.M.	1	For removing catch-pins, also pins axis, sight back, R.S.M.L.E.
Drifts, pin, fixing, stud, head catch, slide, sight, back, R.S.M.L.E.	1	For removing pins fixing.
Drifts, wire, small	1	For removing pins, stop, band lower and band outer.
Drifts, wire, large	1	For removing safety catch, M.L.E.C.L. rifles.
Drivers, Screw :—		
Armourers { large	1	For screws band inner, nose-cap back, guard trigger front, dial sight fixing screw and screw and nut, protector back sight. It is also used for removing the sear spring.
Armourers { small	1	For screws band outer, swivels piling and butt, nose-cap front, disc marking butt, ejector, guard trigger back, sear, spring sight back, stop charger guide, and screw spring sight aperture.

Designation of Tool.	No.	Use of Tool.
Drivers, screw :—		
Extractor, axis, M.L.M.	1	For screws bed back sight, cut off, extractor, keeper fine adjustment, screw nut keeper striker (early marks), and screw wind-gauge, also used for replacing the sear spring.
Fork, dial sight...	1	For screw sight dial pivot, and (with Mk. III and IV Rifles) screw catch slide back.
Implement, action, M.L.E. R. Short.	1	Various uses.
Implement, action, M.L.M.	1	Pattern "D" for M.L.E. charger loading rifles.
Horses, armourers	2	To support rifle.
Hammers, riveting, 4 oz.	1	Various uses.
Pincers, armourers	1	For removing pins or screws that stick after being unscrewed.
Pliers, flat-nose	1	Various uses.
Testers, trigger pull, Mk. II.	1	For weighing various springs.
Tools, adjusting, foresight :—		
Cramps ...	1	Adjusting foresight.
Tools, extractor spring	1	For removing and replacing extractor spring.
Tools removing handguard		
No. 1	1	For removal of rear handguards of all short rifles.
No. 2	1	For removal of handguards of charger loading M.L.E. rifles.
Tools, removing striker :—		
Pattern B.	1	All rifles fitted with strikers, M.L.M.; M.L.M., R.F., No. 2; M.L.E. short, No. 2; and R.F.R.S., No. 2.
Rifle, short, M.L.E.	1	For No. 1 strikers.
Tools removing wad stock bolt	1	For withdrawing the wad stock bolt from the butt.
Tools removing plate keeper screw wind-gauge.	1	For lifting the keeper plate from its recess.

Designation of Tool.	No.	Use of Tool.
Vices standing, 36 lb. ...	1	For holding the rifle while stripping.
Reflectors, mirror, S.A., ·303-inch.	1	For examining barrel.
Gauges, distance of bolt from end of chamber. ·064″	1	For testing minimum distance allowed between face of bolt-head and end of chamber. Must not be used with R.M. ·303″ P/14.
Gauges, distance of bolt from end of chamber. ·074″	1	For testing maximum distance allowed between face of bolt-head and end of chamber. Must not be used with R.M. ·303″ P/14.
Gauges, projection of stock bolt through body.	1	To gauge and ensure that the stock bolt is properly screwed home, and that the projection is not excessive.
Gauge striker point (for height and figure).	1	Protrusion from ·04″—·042″. Radius ·038″.
Pilot pins (not a service store) coned-point, thus—	1	Should be made as required for assisting in the replacement of axis pins for back sights, &c.

GAUGE PLUGS.

The following gauge plugs are used to test the wear of barrels for exchange.

Gauge armourers, plug ·303 inch, ·307 inch, ·308 inch Mark II., ·310 inch, and plug lead No. 2.

Plug ·309 inch and plug lead No. 1 are for use with the Maxim gun.

The following tools are supplied for cleaning barrels and clearing obstructions in the bore such as broken pull-throughs, rust, broken cases in chamber, &c. :—

Designation of Tool.	No.	Use of Tool.
Rods, cleaning, ·303 in. :—		
No. 1	1	For Jute, suitable for long or short rifles.
No. 2	1	For use with brass wire, long rifle. Can be used for M.L.E. rifles, short and P/14, only when fitted with Bush, stop, rod, No. 2.
No. 4	1	For use with brass wire, rifle, short M.L.E. and P/14.
Bush, stop, rod cleaning, ·303, No. 2.	1	For use with rod No. 2 when used with short rifles and P/14.
Muzzle guides :—		
No. 1	1	M.L.E.C.L. rifles. For use when using the above rods to prevent bell-mouthing the muzzle.
No. 2	1	R.S.M.L.E.
No. 3	1	R.M. ·303 in. P/14.
Pull-throughs, Mk. IV. ...	1	Cleaning Bore.
,, ,, double ...	1	Cleaning Bore.
Braces, armourers, bits-screwdriver, stick, cleaning chamber, Mk. II.	1	All Magazine rifles.
Stick, cleaning, chamber, ·303 in. arms, No. 1.	1	For use with Braces, Armourers.
Plugs, plain, ·303 in. arms ...	1	Tapped at end to fit on rod No. 2, for use in removal of bullet envelope, and in tamping when removing a broken pull-through, &c.
Tools, clearing, ·303 in. arms :—		
Bits, screw	1	For removal of broken pull-through, &c.
Bush, bit, screw	1	
Rod, No. 2	1	Screwed at end to take above clearing bits and plugs.
Rods, cleaning, cylinder, pistol, Webley.	1	For use with brass wire.

RIFLE, SHORT MAGAZINE LEE-ENFIELD (MARK III)
Plate I.

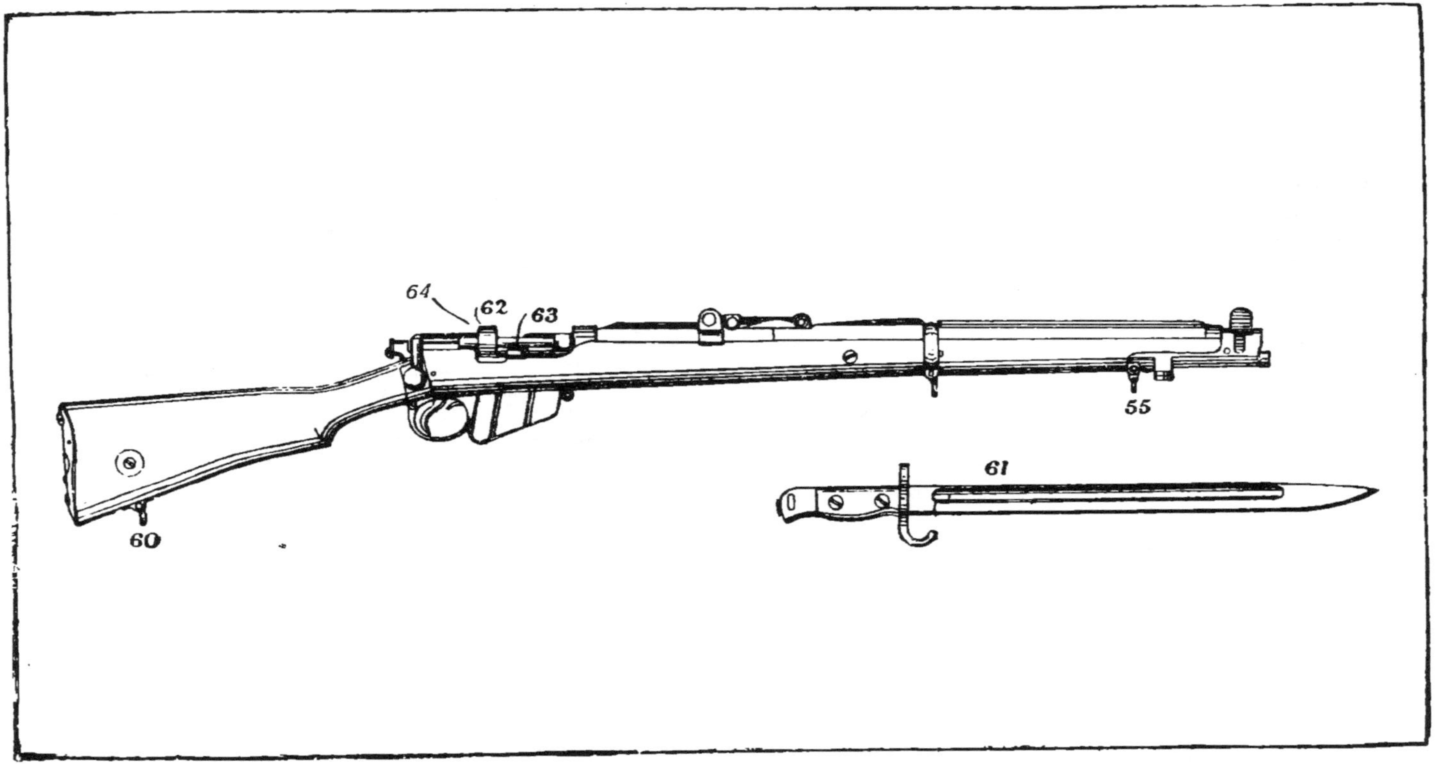

RIFLE, SHORT MAGAZINE LEE-ENFIELD (MARK III)

Plate II.

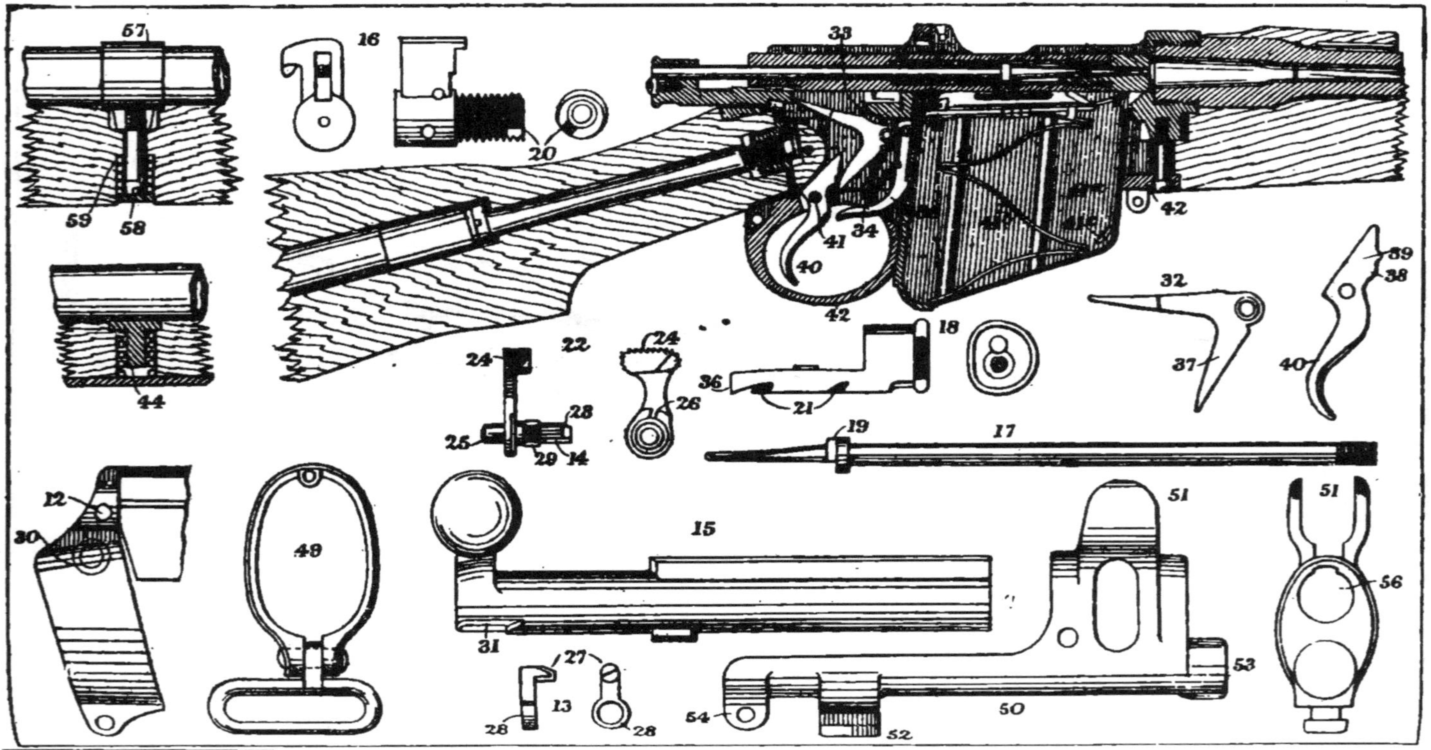

RIFLE, SHORT MAGAZINE LEE-ENFIELD (MARK III)
Plate III.

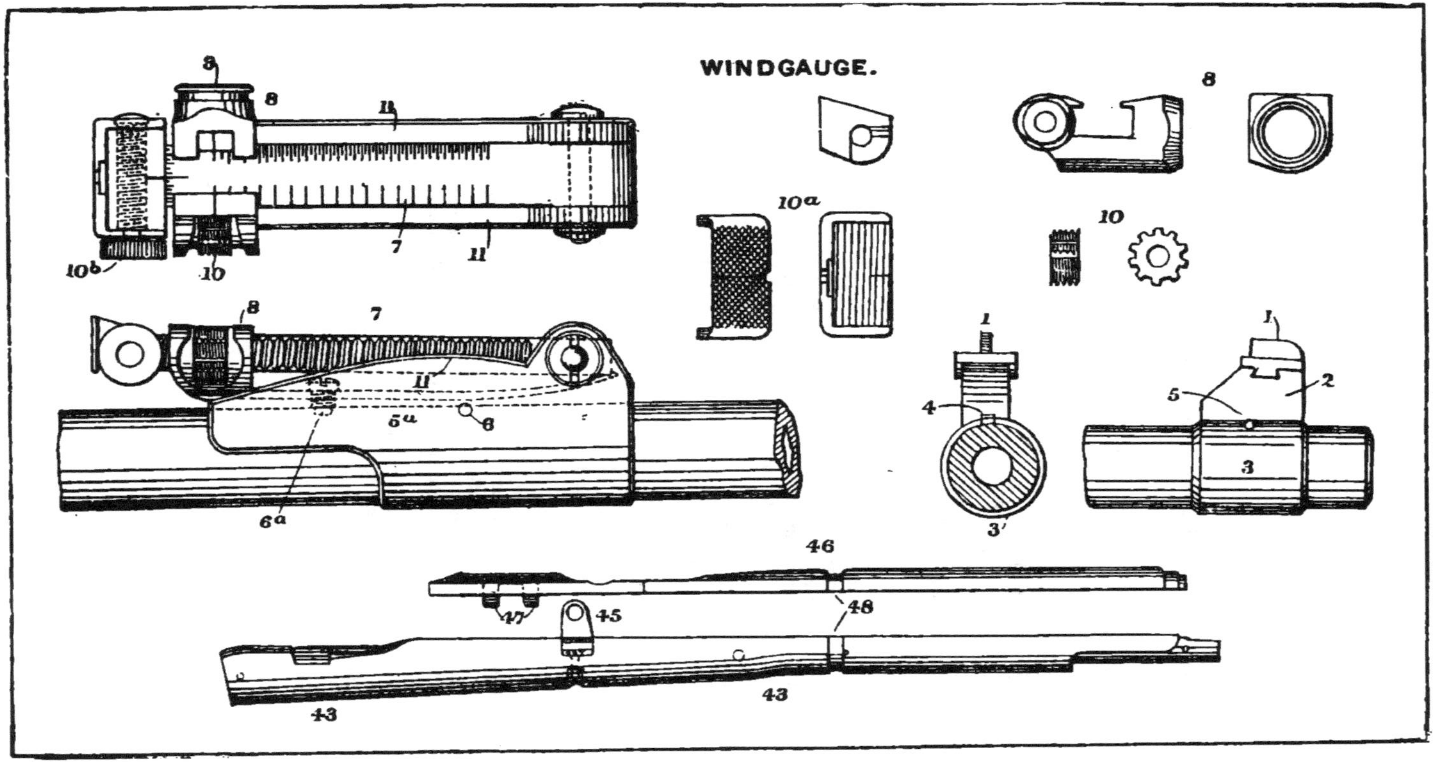

WINDGAUGE.

NAMES OF THE PARTS OF RIFLE, SHORT M.L.E., MARK III REFERRED TO IN PLATES I TO III.

1. Blade foresight.
2. Foresight block.
3. Band foresight block.
4. Key ,, ,,
5. Crosspin ,, ,,
5A. Backsight bed.
6. ,, ,, crosspin.
6A. ,, ,, sight spring screw.
7. Backsight leaf.
8. ,, slide.
9. ,, slide catch.
10. ,, fine adjustment worm wheel.
10A. Wind-gauge.
10B. ,, screw.
11. Backsight ramps.
12. Seating for safety catch.
13. Safety catch.
14. Locking bolt stem.
15. Bolt.
16. ,, head.
17. Striker.
18. Cocking piece.
19. Striker collar with stud.
20. Bolt head tenon.
21. Cocking piece locking recesses.
22. Locking bolt.
23. ,, ,, flat.
24. ,, ,, thumbpiece.
25. ,, ,, aperture sight stem.
26. ,, ,, stop pin recesses.
27. ,, ,, safety catch stem.
28. ,, ,, ,, ,, arm.
29. ,, ,, screw threads.
30. ,, ,, seating.
31. Bolt cam grooves.
32. Sear.
33. ,, seating.
34. ,, spring.
35. Magazine catch.
36. Full bent of cocking piece.
37. Short arm of sear.
38. } Trigger ribs.
39. }
40. Trigger.
41. Trigger axis pin.
41A. Magazine case.
41B. ,, platform spring.
41C. ,, auxiliary ,,
42. Guard trigger.
43. Stock fore-end.
44. Spring and stud fore-end.
45. Protector backsight.
46. Handguard front and rear.
47. Spring handguard rear.
48. Lower band groove.
49. Lower band.
50. Nosecap.
51. Protector foresight.
52. Sword bar.
53. Boss for ring of sword bayonet crosspiece.
54. Swivel seating.
55. ,, piling.
56. Nosecap barrel opening.
57. Inner band.
58. ,, ,, screw.
59. ,, ,, ,, spring.
60. Butt sling swivel.
61. Sword bayonet, pattern 07.
62. Bridge charger guide.
63. Cut-off.
64. Screw ejector.

STRIPPING AND ASSEMBLING.

Rifles, Short, Magazine Lee-Enfield.

Hold the Rifle in the Left Hand.

Remove.	Detail.
Handguard, rear	Raise sight, use Tool No. 1 as a lever, and assist to ease off with fingers and thumb of left hand.

Note.—Great care must be used to avoid splitting the guard.

1st POSITION.

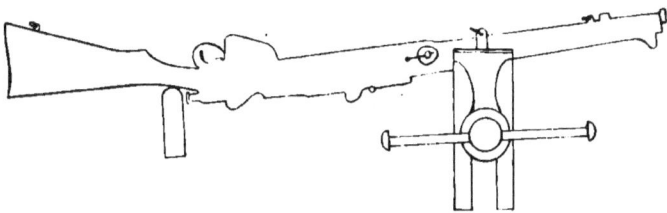

Supported on the left horse underneath the grip and clamped at the band outer clear of the dial sight.

Stripping.

Remove.	Detail.
* Screws, nose-cap, back and front.	Weaker screw removed last.
Nose-cap	With a suitable piece of wood applied against sword-bar tap off towards muzzle.
† Screw, band, outer, and swivel.	
Band, outer, and handguard, front.	Unclamp vice and raise muzzle end.

Assembling.

In reverse order.

Note.--

† Short side of swivels should be on the same side as the dial sight.

* Keep the rear end of nose-cap down to ensure screws engaging correctly.

2ND POSITION.

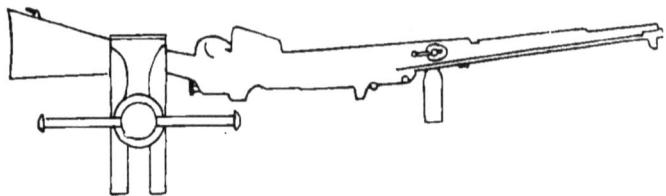

Supported on the right horse just in front of the bed backsight and clamped at the parallel portion of stock butt.

Stripping.

Remove.	Detail.
* Screw, band, inner, and spring	Mark III rifles, unscrew only, remove after fore-end is taken away from barrel.
† Magazine	Release magazine catch.
‡ Screws, guard trigger, front and back	Weaker screw removed last.
Guard, trigger, with trigger	Lift out of seating.
§ Stock, fore-end, with stud and spring	To be lifted level, raising the front end through medium of spring and stud fore-end. If necessary, adopt the method detailed for "removing a tight fore-end."

Note.—For stripping or assembling magazine, *see* p. 20; fore-end, *see* p. 19.

Assembling.

In reverse order.

Note.—

§ Carefully examine fore-end to see that all its fittings are in position. See that the square end on stock bolt is correct and the inner band adjusted before attempting to place fore-end on. If necessary, adopt the method detailed for "replacing a tight fore-end."

‡ Fix the "back screw" first.

† That the stop clip on Nos. 1, 2, and 3 magazines is turned up before attempting to replace.

* Spring, inner, band, should have slight play when the screw is tightened up (test by pressure with large screwdriver).

3RD POSITION.

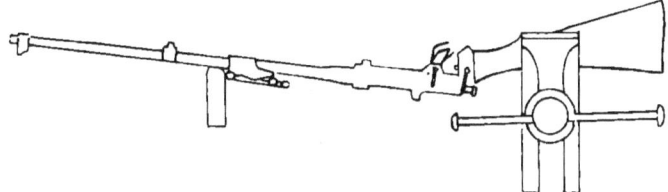

Supported on the left horse just in front of the bed backsight and clamped at the parallel portion of stock butt.

Stripping.

Remove.	Detail.
* Spring, sear	Place large screwdriver between magazine catch and spring, and turn counter-clockwise.
Screw, sear, with spring retaining breech bolt.	
Sear.	
Pin, catch magazine and catch	Using Drift, catch pin, tap out away from bench.
† Screw, cut-off.	
Cut-off	In the open position, ease out by applying screwdriver between the arm of cut-off and body.
Screws, butt plate and plate.	
Wad, stock bolt ...	Use Tool, removing.
‡ Bolt, stock	The body should be held whilst unscrewing bolt. Immediately the bolt jumps, indicating it is free, stop turning, otherwise the square end of the bolt will damage the threads.
§ Body, with barrel, &c.	If necessary, adopt the method detailed for "removing a tight butt."

Assembling.

Note.— In reverse order.

§ If necessary, adopt the method detailed for "replacing a tight butt."

‡ Hold the body correctly against the stock butt, otherwise the square end of bolt will damage the thread in the socket. The bolt to be left *square* and correct to *gauge*. Do not use undue force or the face of socket will probably be distorted. If necessary, use adjusting washers.

† Screw down flush.

* Engage the long arm with the notch on sear, then place a screwdriver against the nib on the short arm, and press gently down until it engages the notch on the magazine catch.

4th Position.

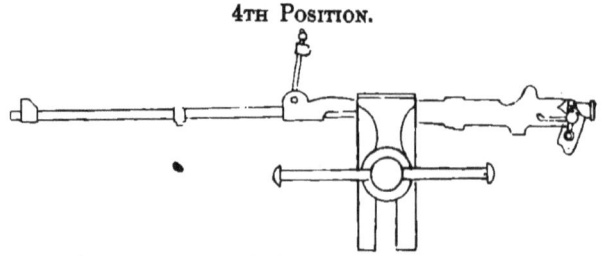

Sight raised, clamp barrel firmly between bed backsight, and reinforce.

Stripping.

Remove.	Detail.
Screw, spring, sight aperture, and spring.	
Sight, aperture.	
* Bolt, locking, with safety catch	Remove and unscrew safety catch from locking bolt.
† Bolt, breech	Raise the bolt lever as far as possible, draw bolt back as far as possible, turn bolt head upwards; the bolt may then be drawn clear.
Note.—For stripping or assembling Bolt, breech, *see* p. 21.	
	Rifles fitted with sliding charger guides necessitate the guide being drawn to the rear to allow the bolt head to be turned vertical.
Sight	*Only to be removed for special instruction or repair.*
Pin, fixing washer, and washer	Use Drift, pin fixing washer. *Note.*—This pin is tapered.
‡ Pin, axis, sight, back, and sight	Use Drift, magazine, catch pin.
Screw, spring, sight, back	Use Driver, screw, Extractor, axis.
Spring, sight, back ...	Dovetailed in; a special tool required to remove it.
Note.—For stripping or assembling backsight, *see* p. 22 or 23.	*Note.*—The bed backsight and the block band foresight are not to be interfered with.

Assembling.

Note.— In reverse order.

‡ Replaced from left to right, using a pilot pin to give it a lead.
† See that the bolt head is screwed home, that the cocking piece, resisting lug, and extractor are all in the vertical plane. Insert the bolt, pushing it forward until bolt head is clear of resisting shoulder, turn bolt head down, draw back the bolt as far as possible, and press head right down ready to engage rib on body. Force bolt home and turn lever right down.

* Place catch on stem of locking bolt at 9 o'clock. Use no

force whatever, and be careful to prevent the catch from sagging when trying to engage the threads. When screwed home correctly it should be at 10.30.

To Remove a Tight Fore-End.

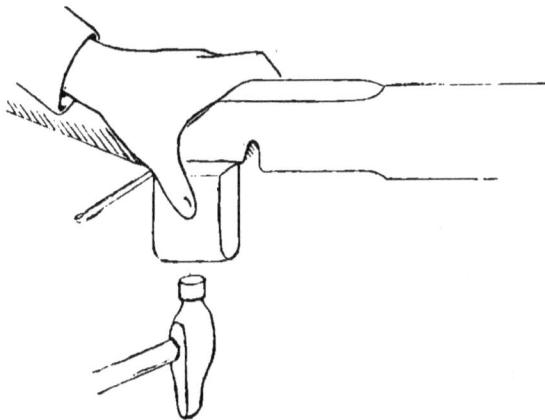

Turn aperture sight clear. Place drift so that its square end bears evenly on sight seating and grip as illustrated above. Tap lightly and pull upwards at the same time.

To Replace a Tight Fore-end.

Place drift in the trigger guard recess, with its slot clearing the magazine catch and evenly supported on the shoulders. Tapping lightly on drift will cause fore-end to bear correctly on body.

Note.—Fore-ends generally project above the socket, therefore to ascertain if the fore-end is home, look inside the magazine way.

To Remove a Tight Stock Butt.

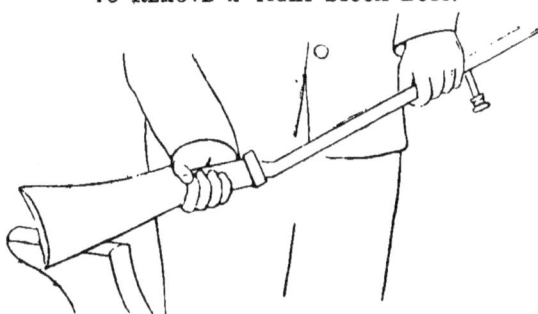

Grasp the rifle as illustrated. Then tap the butt smartly, about 3 inches from the heel, on the shoulder of the right horse, at the same time pulling outwards with both hands.

The greatest care must be taken to ensure that the stock bolt is free of the body before doing this.

This can be ascertained by inspection, and, if necessary, pressure with a drift inserted from the front of the stock bolt hole in body.

To Assemble a Tight Stock Butt.

Fix the stock correctly into the socket. Hold the rifle with the left hand, muzzle pointing downwards, and place the "anvil" so that it lies evenly on the butt. Drive the butt home by tapping smartly on the anvil.

To Remove the Backsight only.

Remove.	Detail.
Handguard, rear...	Raise sight. Use Tool No. 1 as a lever and assist to ease off with fingers and thumb of left hand.
Band, outer	Rifle to be fixed in the 1st Position.
Handguard, front	Rest butt on the floor and slide handguard down clear of nose-cap and remove.
Sight	Use cork clams to prevent damaging fore-end. Fix rifle in the 4th Position and proceed as detailed on p. 16.

Note.—To strip the sight, *see* p. 22 or 23.

STRIPPING AND ASSEMBLING COMPONENTS.
Rifle, Short, Magazine Lee-Enfield.

FORE-END.

Held lightly in the vice.

Stripping.

Remove.	Detail.
Screw, dial sight, pivot	Use Driver, screw, Fork, dial sight.
* Spring.	
Pointer.	
Screw, fixing dial sight	Unscrew three complete turns. Then tap lightly on head of screw to loosen dial plate. Complete unscrewing and remove.
Dial plate	
Nut and screw protector, backsight	(Marks III and IV rifles only.) Hold screw whilst unscrewing nut.
† Protector, backsight.	

Assembling.

In reverse order.

Note.—

† Bowed wing to be on the right side of fore-end.
* Concave face outwards.
That the following fittings are in position :—

    Plate, keeper, stock bolt.
    Collar, screw, front, trigger guard.
    Washer, nut screw, protector, backsight.
    Washer, screw, fixing dial sight.
    Washer, spring, band, inner.
    Nut, screw, back, nose-cap.
    Stud with spring, fore-end.

MAGAZINES NOS. 1, 2, AND 3.

Stripping.

Right side uppermost.

Remove.	Detail.
Platform with spring ...	Turn the stop clip to front of magazine. Depress rear end of platform and draw the front end clear of magazine behind the front lip. Then ease platform out to the front, twisting it slightly to the right.
Auxiliary spring... ...	Ease off the front of case.

Assembling.

Reverse the motions used in removing. It will be found to assist the rear end of platform into place if it be slightly twisted to the right when being inserted.

MAGAZINE NO. 4.

Stripping.

Remove.	Detail.
Platform with spring ...	Depress the rear end of the platform as far as possible, at the same time holding up the front end; then pull the front end towards the rear end of case until it passes under the front side lips and between the inner forward ribs of the case through which it is sprung. Raise the front end of platform out of the case and tilt the rear end sideways—left side uppermost—and draw forward out of case.
Auxiliary spring	Ease off the front of case.

Assembling.

Reverse the motions used in removing.

BOLT BREECH.

Stripping.

Remove.	Detail.
Screw, stop, charger, guide.	(Marks I, I*, II, and II* rifles.)
* Spring, extractor ...	Use punch end of Tool, removing. Cover with thumb to prevent spring flying out.
Screw, extractor.	
Extractor.	
Screw, keeper, striker.	Use a suitable coin or screwdriver.
† Bolt head, with striker, mainspring, and cocking piece.	See that the stud on cocking piece is in the long cam.

Note.—If it is found that the striker is not unscrewing with the bolt head, draw back the cocking piece clear of cams, and turn till its stud rests on rear end of bolt, then screw home the bolt head, lower the cocking piece until its stud rests in the long cam, and complete the unscrewing of the striker from the cocking piece with the bolt head.

If the striker is tight in the cocking piece, probably the bolt head cannot be moved together with the striker, in which case the striker should be hung up as above whilst the bolt head is removed, afterwards removing the striker with the "Tool, removing."

If undue force is used when attempting to unscrew by means of the bolt head, the striker lug recess and thread on tenon of bolt head are liable to damage.

N.B.—If fitted with striker M.L.E.R.S. Mk. I, No. 2, *see* p. 28.

Assembling.

† Place spring on striker and replace in bolt. Engage bolt head and striker and screw striker partly home.

Place cocking piece in position with stud in long cam and continue screwing. If, when bolt head is screwed home, the shoulder formed on end of striker is not *flush* with the bottom of the recess in the end of cocking piece, withdraw and hang up cocking piece (as explained in stripping), unscrew the bolt head several turns, let the cocking piece go forward again into the long cam, and continue screwing. Replace the keeper screw, being careful that the cut-away portion of the striker is in the correct position.

Note.—It is essential that the bolt head should be correctly screwed home, otherwise the bolt will jam when trying to close the breech.

* To prevent breaking this spring, see that it is properly fitted into its seating before attempting to engage the stud (liable to slip down into the extractor seating).

Backsight, Marks III and IV.

Stripping.

Remove.	Detail.
Screw, catch, slide, b.s., and spring.	Use Driver, screw, Fork, dial sight.
Slide, with catch slide...	Press in catch to disengage worm from rack and draw slide off leaf.
Catch, slide, with worm, f.a., from slide	Using Drift, press catch with worm outwards.
Pin, axis, worm, and worm	(Repair only.) Cylindrical pin.
Pin, fixing head, screw, wind-gauge	Use Drift, pin, fixing head, screw. *Note.*—This pin is tapered.
* Head screw, wind-gauge.	
† Spring, head screw.	
‡ Screw, wind-gauge.	Use Driver, screw, Extractor, axis.
Wind-gauge.	
Spring, wind-gauge.	

Assembling.

In reverse order.

Note.—

‡ A washer screw wind-gauge may be fitted to take up backlash.

† That the square ended projection and not the nib engages in the groove in wind-gauge.

* That it is in correct relation with screw wind-gauge to receive the tapered pin.

BACKSIGHT, MARKS I, I*, II, AND II*.

Stripping.

Remove.	Detail.
* Slide, with catch slide from leaf.	Press studs in and draw slide off leaf.
† Catches, slide, with springs from slide.	Draw outwards.
Screw, keeper, fine adjustment.	
‡ Fine adjustment and springs.	Turn screw, fine adjustment, taking care to cover springs with thumb as fine adjustment is moving off the top of leaf.
§ Screw, fine adjustment, with spring.	Lift out of seating.
Plate, keeper, wind-gauge screw.	Lift out of recess with tool.
‖ Screw, wind-gauge, with spring.	Hold wind-gauge whilst turning.
¶ Wind-gauge.	

Assembling.

In reverse order.

Note.—

¶ Concave face inwards.

‖ Adjust spring and press on head of screw to facilitate replacing.

§ Concave face inwards.

‡ Replace springs with points towards fine adjustment. Fix fine adjustment square on top of leaf, keeping a light pressure against the side of the springs. With screwdriver, compress one of the springs and make it engage under fine adjustment. Taking care to retain this spring, compress the other and make it engage in like manner. Keeping the fine adjustment square, press down and forward, to ensure screw engaging correctly.

† Insert together.

* Make sure that slide (especially slide No. 2) is placed correctly on leaf.

STRIPPING AND ASSEMBLING.

Rifles, Charger Loading, M.L.E., Mark I and I*.

Hold the rifle in the left hand.

Remove.	Detail.
Handguard, rear...	Raise sight. Unclamp and move slide to top of leaf. Apply Tool No. 2 as a lever over the bed backsight.

1st Position.

Supported on the left horse underneath the grip, and clamped at the band lower, clear of the dial sight.

Stripping.

Remove.	Detail.
Screw, nose-cap.	
Nose-cap	Tap off clear of fore-end, not taken off the barrel.
Screw, band, lower, and swivel.	
Band, lower	Unclamp vice; with thumb spring band open to clear pins, and slide clear.

Assembling.

In reverse order.

Note.—Short side of swivel on the same side as the dial sight.

2ND POSITION.

Supported on the right horse in front of the bed backsight, and clamped at the parallel portion of the stock butt.

Stripping.

Remove.	Detail.
* Magazine	Release magazine catch.
Screws, guard trigger, front and back	Weaker screw removed last.
† Guard trigger, with trigger.	Lift out of seating.
‡ Fore-end	To be lifted off level. If necessary, adopt the method detailed for " Removing a tight fore-end " (p. 17).

Note.—For stripping or assembling magazine, *see* p. 20; dial sight, *see* p. 19.

Assembling.

In reverse order.

Note.—

‡ That the Plate, keeper, stock bolt, Collar, screw, front, trigger guard, and Washer, screw, fixing dial sight, are in position. That the square end on stock bolt is correct before attempting to place fore-end on. If necessary, adopt the method detailed for " Replacing a tight fore-end " (p. 17).

† That the trigger engages correctly with the sear.

* That the stop clip on Nos. 1, 2, and 3 magazines is turned up correctly before attempting to replace.

3RD POSITION.

Supported on the left horse in front of the bed backsight, and clamped at the parallel portion of the stock butt.

Stripping.

Remove.	Detail.
* Spring, sear	Place large screwdriver between magazine catch and spring, and turn counter-clockwise.
Screw, sear, with spring retaining breech bolt.	
Sear.	
Pin, catch, magazine and catch	Use Drift, catch pin, and tap out away from bench.
† Screw, cut-off.	
Cut-off	In the open position, ease out by applying screwdriver between the arm and body.
Screw, butt plate, and plate.	Turn rifle to remove screw in heel strap.
Wad, stock bolt ...	Use Tool, removing.
‡ Bolt, stock	The body should be held whilst unscrewing bolt. Immediately the bolt jumps, indicating it is free, stop turning, otherwise the square end of bolt will damage the threads.
§ Body, with barrel, &c.	If necessary, adopt the method detailed for " Removing a tight butt " (p. 17).

Assembling.

In reverse order.

Note.—

§ If necessary, adopt the method detailed for "Replacing a tight butt" (p. 18).

‡ Hold the body correctly against the stock butt, otherwise the square end of bolt will damage the thread in the socket. The bolt to be left *square* and correct to *gauge*. Do not use undue force or the face of socket will probably be distorted. If necessary, use adjusting washers.

† Screw down flush.

* Engage the long arm with the notch on sear, then place a screwdriver against the nib on the short arm, and press gently down until it engages the notch on the magazine catch.

4th Position.

Sight raised, clamp firmly at the bed backsight, allowing sufficient clearance to facilitate removal of Pin, axis, backsight.

Stripping.

Remove.	Detail.
Screw, spring, sight aperture, with spring.	
Aperture, sight.	
* Safety catch	Raise to midway position. Use Drift, wire, large, and tap out to the right.
† Screw, keeper, striker	More convenient to remove in this position.
‡ Bolt, breech, with safety pin and spring.	Raise the bolt lever as far as possible, draw bolt back as far as possible, turn bolt head upwards, and draw bolt clear. Carefully remove pin and spring.

Note.—For stripping or assembling bolt breech, *see* p. 28.

Sight	*Only to be removed for special instruction or repair.*
§ Pin, axis, sight, back, and sight.	Use Drift, sight, axis pin, M.L.M.
Screw, spring, sight, back.	Use Driver, screw, Extractor, axis.
Spring, sight, back ...	Dovetailed in, a special tool required to remove it.

Note.—The bed backsight, block, and protector foresight are not to be interfered with.

Note.—For stripping or assembling backsight, *see* p. 29.

Assembling.

In reverse order.

Note.—
  § Replace from left to right.
  ‡ That the bolt head is screwed home, that the cocking piece, resisting lug, and extractor are all in the vertical plane. Insert the bolt, pushing it forward until bolt head is clear of resisting shoulder, turn bolt head down, draw back the bolt as far as possible, and press head right down ready to engage rib on body. Force bolt home and turn lever right down.
  † Complete the screwing up of screw, keeper, striker.
  * That the spring and pin are in position before attempting to replace.

STRIPPING AND ASSEMBLING COMPONENTS.

Rifles, Charger Loading, M.L.E., Mark I and I*.

BOLT BREECH.

Stripping.

Remove.	Detail.
* Spring, extractor	Use punch end of Tool, removing, cover with thumb to prevent flying out.
Screw, extractor.	
Extractor.	
† Screw, keeper, striker	*Note.*—Easier to take out with the bolt in the rifle.
Bolt head	Unscrew.
‡ Striker, with main spring and cocking piece	Stud of cocking piece in long cam. With Tool, removing, unscrew striker.

Assembling.

Note.—

‡ Replace main spring and striker. Place cocking piece in position and screw the striker home until the shoulder formed on end of striker is flush with the bottom of the keeper screw recess and the cut away part correctly adjusted to receive the head of the keeper screw.

† Screw in sufficiently to retain striker in the correct position. (Screw home after replacing in rifle.)

* To prevent breaking this spring, see that it is properly fitted into its seating before attempting to engage the stud (liable to slip down into the extractor seating).

MARK I* BACKSIGHT (FITTED WITH No. 1 SLIDE).

Stripping.

Remove.	Detail.
Screw, stop	Use Driver, screw, Extractor, axis.
* Slide from leaf... ...	Release clamping nut.
† Nut, clamping, slide ...	Press stud clear and unscrew.
† Stud, clamping, slide ...	Ease out of recess.
Pin fixing head screw, wind-gauge	Use Drift, pin fixing head screw. *Note.*—This pin is tapered.
‡ Head screw, wind-gauge	Draw off.
Screw, wind-gauge ...	Use Driver, screw, Extractor, axis.
Wind-gauge from slide.	
§ Spring, wind-gauge.	
Spring, slide	Spring out of seating.

Note —With No. 2 slides (identified by the head screw being the same size as the clamping nut) the nut, clamping, and stud are not removed until after the spring, wind-gauge, and are replaced accordingly.

Assembling.

In reverse order.

Note.—

§ Convex side up.

‡ That it is in correct relation with screw to receive its tapered pin.

† Insert stud, roughened face inwards.

Screw on. These components are correctly assembled when the nut is screwed until its projection is just past the stud and is prevented from unscrewing by the stud when the face of the latter is flush with the inner face of slide.

* Press stud, clamping, outwards to give clearance.

ACTION OF MECHANISM—R.S.M.L.E. AND C.L. RIFLES.

Assuming that the rifle has just been fired, there are four distinct motions of the bolt necessary before another round is ready to be fired.

(1) *Raising the Bolt Lever.*—The bolt is revolved, but the cocking piece and bolt head are prevented from turning, the former by the groove in the body, the latter by its hook engaging the rib on the body. Consequently the cam-shaped face between the long and short grooves of the bolt bears against the stud on the cocking piece, and forces the cocking piece to the rear, thus withdrawing the striker from the cartridge and slightly compressing the mainspring from the front. At the same time, owing to the cam face on the bolt lug acting against the face of

the extracting cam recess in the body, the bolt is drawn back with a powerful motion, the extractor moves in and engages with the cartridge and primary extraction of the cartridge is effected. The long rib on the bolt is now opposite the rib-way in the body, and the stud on the cocking piece is in the short groove.

(2) *Drawing back the Bolt.*—The cartridge is extracted and ejected by the action of the shallowing groove and ejector screw on the left side of the body. The bolt is brought up by the projection on the bolt head coming against the resistance shoulder of the body.

(3) *Pushing forward the Bolt.*—The face of the bolt head engages with the top cartridge in the magazine (or with the round placed in by hand) and pushes it into the chamber. The full bent on the cocking piece engages with the sear, and the mainspring is compressed from the rear. The stud between the grooves on the bolt passes on the right of the stud on the cocking piece.

(4) *Turning down the Bolt Lever.*—The bolt lug and the long rib, engaging respectively with the sloping recess in the body and the resistance shoulder, force the bolt forward against the base of the cartridge. The cartridge is now firmly supported, the mainspring is fully compressed, the action is at full cock, and the stud on the cocking piece is opposite the long groove in the bolt.

Pressing the Trigger.

The sear is revolved, at first with a slower and more powerful motion and then with a quicker motion, the bents are disengaged, and the striker flies forward and fires the cartridge.

(The charger loading rifle has only one motion in the pull-off instead of a double motion action.)

Safety Arrangements.

(1) Locking bolt and safety-catch.

To prevent the rifle being fired accidentally (and to prevent loss of bolts on line of march, particularly with M.I.).

(2) Studs on cocking piece and rear end of bolt, and half bent in cocking piece engaging on sear.

To prevent the rifle being fired with the bolt not properly closed.

In this case, either (*a*) the stud on cocking piece coming against sloping face of stud on bolt, automatically closes the bolt; or (*b*) stud on cocking piece strikes full against stud on bolt. If the bolt is then closed, the sear engages in the half-bent, and the action is locked, as the two studs are side by side The action must be re-cocked by pulling back the cocking piece by hand.

WEIGHING OF SPRINGS.

Method of Weighing.—A spring balance, called a "Tester, trigger, pull" (T.T.P.), is supplied for the purpose of weighing all the springs, upon the correctness of which, in conjunction with cleanliness of the parts, depends the accurate and smooth working of the breech action. If a vice is available it should be used in preference to any other arrangement, as more accurate results are obtained. Once the rifle is fixed in the vice, its position need not be changed, as all the springs can be weighed in that position as described below.

Position in the Vice.—Remove the handguard, rear, so as not to split it with the jaws of the vice.

Secure the rifle immediately in rear of the bed backsight, in a horizontal position, the muzzle pointing towards the left, and the right side up.

Note.—The magazine must always be in position.

Now fully cock the mechanism and proceed as follows.

Pull off.—(The pressure required to release the sear from the full bent of cocking-piece.)

Place the friction roller of the T.T.P. over the finger piece of the trigger, and holding the other end in the right hand, pull in a line diagonally across the small of the butt, steadying the right hand on the back of the left, the finger tips of latter resting on the butt near the heel.

A steady pull should be given, and when the trigger begins to move the weight should be from 3 to 4 lbs.; continue the pull, and when the striker is released the balance should show 5 to 6 lbs. (Rifles short, double pull.)

Charger Loading Rifles.—Pull to move trigger when mainspring is eased $3\frac{1}{4}$ to $4\frac{1}{2}$ lbs., pull off 5 to 7 lbs. (Single pull.)

Note.—The above results are only obtained when the components of the action, including the trigger, are clean and free from oil, or other matter, causing obstruction.* The action should, therefore, be thoroughly cleaned, and slightly oiled; special attention being paid to the following:—(1) That the mainspring is the correct weight. (2) That the bent on the cocking piece and the ribs on the trigger (short rifles) have not been damaged. (3) That there is no packing or foreign substance on the sear seat in the body. (4) That the sear screw is not bent.

If all these points have been attended to and it is still found that the weight is outside the limits laid down, the rifle should be returned to store for special examination.

---

* The action may appear free from oil, but if there is an accumulation of dirty or thick oil in the mainspring chamber, in the bolt hole of the cocking piece, or in striker hole in the bolt head, miss-fires are likely to occur.

Mainspring.—(1) With the striker in the fired position, place the tag of the T.T.P. over the end of the cocking piece, and pull in a direct line with the bolt. When the cocking piece moves the weight should be from 7 to 9 lbs. (2) Cock the action, test again in a similar way, when the weight should be from 14 to 16 lbs.

Spring retaining Bolt Head.—(1) Draw back the bolt until the head is over the spring retaining. (2) Place the claws of tag round the bolt head, and pull with the T.T.P. slightly below the horizontal, and at right angles to the bolt; when the bolt head is released from the spring the weight should be from 10 to 16 lbs. If the weight is outside these limits examine the sear screw and see if it is home and tight.

Extractor Spring.—With the bolt head released, as by the last operation, place the tip of one of the claws of T.T.P. under the hook of the extractor and pull against its spring; when the extractor moves the weight should be from $4\frac{1}{2}$ to $5\frac{1}{2}$ lbs., *if fitted with a spring numbered "3," 7 to 9 lbs.*

Trap Butt Spring.—Place the tip of the claw under the nib of trap butt; to move the latter the weight should be from 2 to 3 lbs. (converted rifles, and rifles charger loading, $3\frac{1}{2}$ to $4\frac{1}{2}$ lbs.).

Springs do not gain strength; therefore, if too heavy, look for burrs, dirt, or other cause of friction.

MISS-FIRES AND FAILURES.

Assuming that the ammunition is good, these may be placed under the following headings, viz. :—

- *A.* Miss-fires.
- *B.* Non-Extraction or Bad Ejection.
- *C.* Light or Heavy pull-off.
- *D.* Defective Magazine Supply.

A. Miss-fires.—Probably due to:—(1) Rusty, weak, or broken mainspring. (2) Bent or broken striker. (3) Insufficient protrusion, owing to (*a*) point of striker worn, (*b*) striker screwed too far into cocking piece, (*c*) rust or grit in front of striker, or damaged hole in bolt head, (*d*) wrong pattern keeper screw, viz., a M.L.M. screw in a M.L.E. cocking piece, (*e*) stud on cocking piece or long groove in bolt burred up, (*f*) thick or dirty oil in mainspring chamber, in striker hole in bolt head, or in bolt hole of cocking piece. (4) Bolt not properly closed. (5) Bolt or body badly worn or indented at recoil shoulders.

B. Non-Extraction or Bad Ejection.—Probably due to:—(1) Rusty, dirty, or scored chamber. (2) Broken extractor, weak or broken extractor spring. (3) Hook of extractor worn. (4) Extractor screw hole enlarged or screw worn small. (5) Ejector screw worn. (6) Wrong pattern of extractor spring. (7) Bolt head very loose in bolt.

C. Light Pull-off.—Probably due to :—(1) Light mainspring. (2) Light sear spring. (3) Dirt or packing on the sear seat. (4) Striker not screwed home. (5) Sear too low, or the magazine not in position. (6) Improper form of bent of cocking piece. (7) Screw, guard trigger, front, not properly screwed up.

Heavy Pull-off.—Probably due to :—(1) Main or sear spring too heavy. (2) Sear too high. (3) A bent sear screw. (4) Magazine not pushed home to the correct position, *i.e.*, the bent on the magazine catch not engaging with the bent on the magazine case, and consequently the sear spring unduly compressed. (5) Improper form of bent of cocking piece.

D. Defective Magazine Supply.—Generally due to :—(1) Platform spring weak or broken. (2) Distorted platform. (3) Magazine case dented or rusted. (4) Magazine not engaged by the catch. (5) Damaged cartridges.

Inaccurate Shooting.

As far as the rifle is concerned, this would be due probably to some of the following causes :—

(1) Front or back sight not correctly adjusted or sight slide wrongly assembled (reversed).
(2) Badly rusted or enlarged bore.
(3) Bent, bulged or dented barrel.
(4) Warped fore-end or handguard.
(5) Fore-end or nose-cap incorrectly adjusted.
(6) Wrong bolt.

With regard to (5), the fore-end and nose-cap are carefully adjusted to each rifle, and play of ·002" is allowed between the barrel and nose-cap, and between the barrel and inner band. The nose-cap and fore-end are both given the same number as the rifle.

With regard to (6), the bolt is carefully adjusted to each rifle, and given the same number as the rifle. Bolts must always be used with the particular rifle to which they are numbered for the following reasons:—The shock on discharge is taken up by the longitudinal rib on the bolt, supported by the resistance shoulder, and at the same time by the lug on the underside of the bolt, supported by the rear wall of the cam recess in the body. Therefore if the shock of discharge is not evenly divided between these two supports, the shooting will be erratic; the shot going towards the left if the resistance shoulder takes the greater part of shock and vice versa.

EXAMINATION OF SHORT AND CHARGER LOADING RIFLES.

(Remove handguards, front and rear, *see* p. 18 or 24.)

Number of Rifle.—Should be the same on: Bolt lever, body, barrel, sight leaf, and, in short rifles, fore-end and nose-cap.

Barrel.—Remove bolt, thoroughly clean barrel, and examine. Internally for: Cordwear, bends, bulges, cuts, rust, metallic fouling, excessive scoring, erosion, or other damage. Externally for: Rust and condition of browning.

Nose-cap.—Examine: Boss, for deposit of nickel, burrs, &c.; sword bar, for burrs; screws; front and back, to see that they are tight; screws, swivel, tight, and inserted from left to right.

Spring Stud, Fore-end.—Should be free, and should keep the barrel in contact with the top of the elliptical opening in nose-cap. To test, place the point of a dummy cartridge bullet in the muzzle and rock, when there should be a slight movement, and the muzzle should be returned to the top of the opening by the spring.

Spring Band, Inner.—To be free. Test by pressing with a large screwdriver, against the screw, resting the rifle against something rigid; if correct, a slight movement should be felt. If the screw is not free it is generally due to an excess of wood.

Trigger Guard.—Screws home and fast.

Stock Butt.—Firmly attached to body.

Butt Plate.—Screws tight.

Butt Swivel.—Screw tight.

Furniture.—Examine woodwork generally.

Pull-through.—Weight not damaged, and cord in good condition.

Oil Bottle.—Correct.

*Sights.**

Foresight.—Securely fixed, and in good condition.

Backsight.—The bed should be firm, the leaf firm at the joint, it must work smoothly, and the spring must be in good order. See that the slide is assembled correctly on the leaf, that it works smoothly, and that the catches engage truly with the racks. The fine adjustment and wind gauge should fit firmly and move smoothly. See that the ramps are not damaged With Mark III and converted Mark IV see that the worm teeth are not damaged, and that they engage truly with the rack when the catch is released. Also with these marks see that the protector backsight has the chequered edges towards the breech or its cranked wing on the right to permit extreme right traverse to the wind-gauge.

Dial Sight.—See that the screw fixing and screw pivot are tight, that the pointer is not bent, and that the spring affords it

---

*Note.—Rifles, charger loading M.L.E., Mark I, are not provided with adjustable fore-sights, sight protector and screw, or wind-gauges on the slide of the back-sight.

the correct stiffness of movement, that the bead is in good condition, and that the plate is of the correct pattern.

Aperture Sight.—See that the screw is tight, that the sight is not bent or damaged, and that the spring holds it in the correct positions.

Carefully wipe barrel and lubricate with composition; examine and replace handguards, outer band, swivel and screw.

Swivel, and band screws, go in from left to right.

Screws must not be loosened to give freedom to a moving part; if this appears to be necessary the fitting is at fault.

Sword Bayonet.—The sword bayonet when properly fitted should have the bolt in the pommel flush with the exterior of the pommel, and the bolt engaging truly with its bearings on the standard, or sword bar of the nose-cap. Should the bolt project beyond the pommel, whether fixed or unfixed, it indicates that grit or dirt has accumulated in the bolt hole, or lodged upon the shoulder bearings for the bolt in the pommel; the sword bayonet would be thereby prevented from being firmly fixed or locked. If the bolt is flush with the pommel when unfixed, and projects when fixed, the end of the pommel is probably bearing on the nose-cap in the case of sword bayonets pattern 1888, and in the case of sword bayonets pattern 1903 and 1907, the rounded end of the sword bar is fouling the socket in the bayonet. This would cause the sword bayonet to be loose, and liable to drop off. This defect should be attended to by an armourer.

Weigh all springs, as detailed on pp. 28, 29.

For testing of barrels for wear, *see* p. 34.

The Action.

Gas Escapes.—Should be clear.

Cartridge Lead.—Examine condition.

Extractor Seating.—Examine condition.

Safety Catch and Locking Bolt.—Should work smoothly and be held in the locked and unlocked positions (showing that the studs on body, recesses in safety catch and spring aperture sight are correct). See that the inner ends of the safety catch and locking bolt are not unduly worn or burred. See that the safety arrangements are in correct working order. To ascertain this proceed as follows:—(1) Turn the safety catch to the rear and see if the bolt is safely locked, turn to the front and fully cock by opening and closing the breech. (2) Try the safety catch in this position; now place the locking bolt in the mid-way position and press the trigger, when the striker should hang up; now push the safety bolt fully to the firing position; this should release the striker, and as the cocking piece moves to the front the sear nose should engage with the half bent.

Note.—If this action takes place correctly it shows that the sear is standing at its proper angle, and also that there is no danger of premature firing owing to worn full bents.

Body.—Examine for burrs, &c., especially in the cocking piece groove, bolt way, and extracting cam recess.

Trigger and Sear.—See that the sear nose engages the half and full bents on the cocking piece correctly, and that it clears the lug on the bolt.

Bolt Breech.—(1) See that it works freely. (2) See that the striker is correctly secured in the cocking piece by its keeper screw. Test the striker point for protrusion and figure (place stud on cocking piece in long cam on bolt and use pattern "C" gauge), protrusion ·04 inch to ·042 inch. See that the striker works easily in the bolt. To do this close the breech and ease the striker, place the thumb of right hand on the knob of lever, and press the trigger with the forefinger; then with the thumb and forefinger of left pull the cocking piece backward and forward. Note if the stud on cocking piece is rubbing against the walls of the long cam. If so, the rifle must be returned to store for adjustment (this defect would probably cause a miss-fire). (3) See that the cocking piece is not too loose on the striker and that its bents are in good condition and not burred, and that the locking recesses are in good order. (4) See that the extractor hook is not broken or unduly worn and that the extractor screw is tight and the head not damaged. (5) That the bolt is not burred or in any way damaged. (6) See that the bolt head is correctly screwed home. (7) See that the bolt closes over the ·064 gauge and that it will not close over the ·074 gauge. (8) Charger guide where present should not be over-loose but work freely.

Feed Mechanism.

Magazine Platform and Catch.—Examine case for dents, &c., noting condition of lips and stop clip. See that the platform rises freely. The magazine catch should stand flush with guide ribs on the trigger guard and its bent should be in good condition. Test by placing the magazine in position.

Feed and Cut-off.—Load the magazine with ten dummy cartridges fed from chargers. Work the action by closing and opening the breech and see that the magazine feeds properly. Open and close the cut-off to see that it works freely and that its projection prevents it from turning clear of slot in body.

Primary Extraction and Ejection.—Test by loading empty cases separately by hand. See that they are ejected properly and that the ejector screw is flush with level of bolt groove.

Note.—Fired cases should be used so that they shall offer the requisite resistance to withdrawal.

PLATE IV.

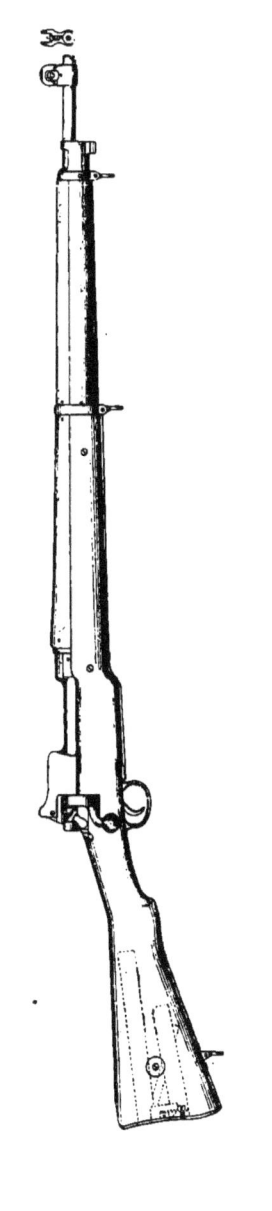

RIFLE, MAGAZINE, .303 INCH, PATTERN 1914

PLATE V.

RIFLE, MAGAZINE, .303 INCH, PATTERN 1914.

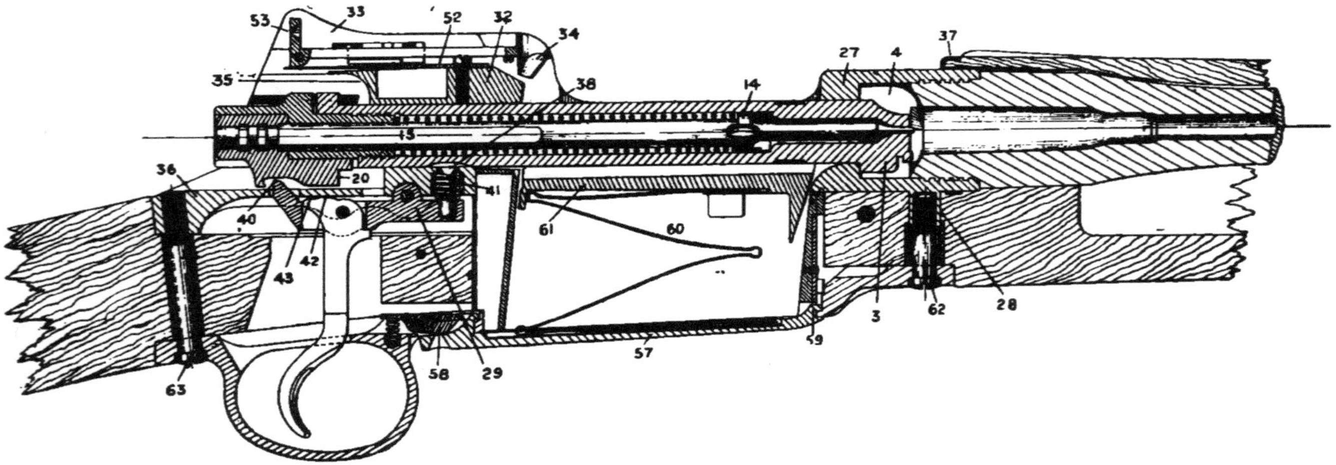

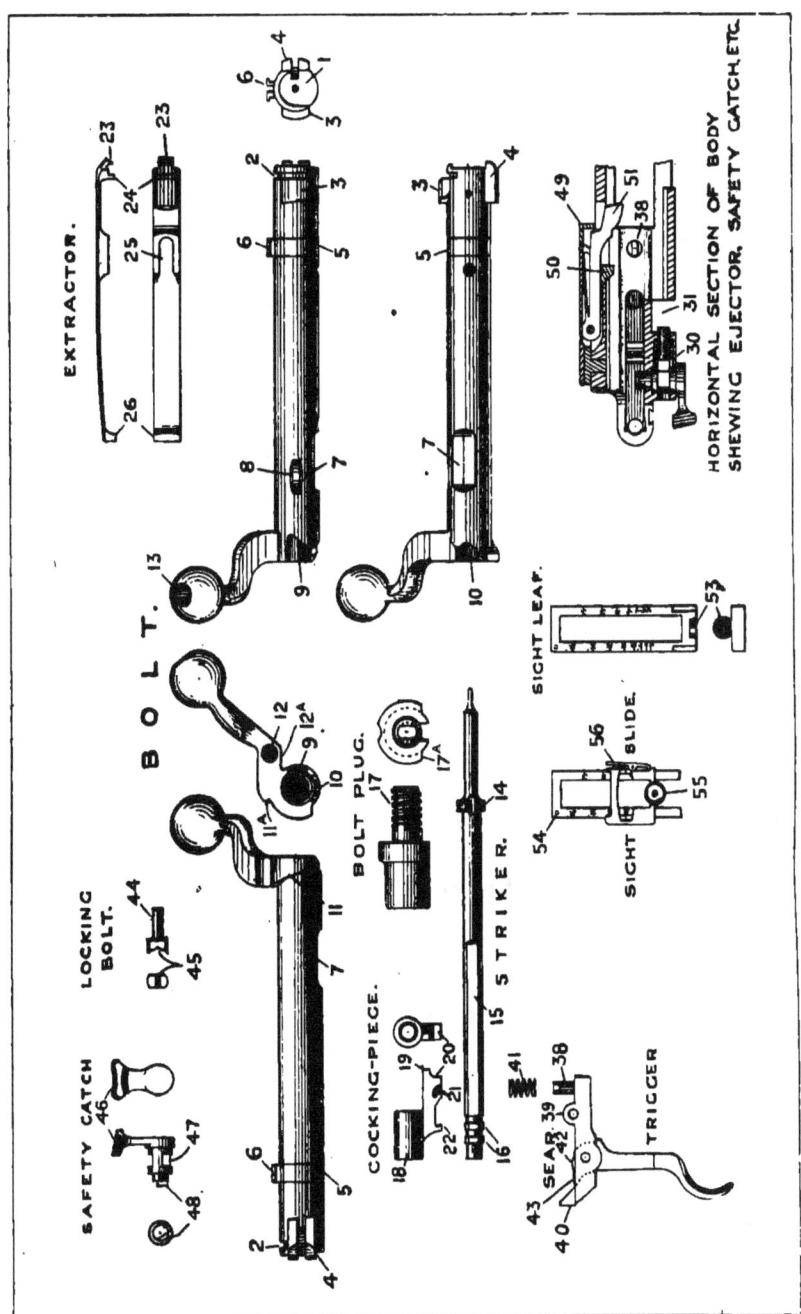

NAMES OF THE PARTS OF RIFLE, MAGAZINE, ·308-inch, PATTERN 1914.
ILLUSTRATED IN PLATES IV. TO VI.

1. Bolt, front face.
2. ,, cannelure.
3. ,, solid lug.
4. ,, split lug.
5. ,, recess for ring.
6. ,, lugs on ring.
7- ,, depression for safety stud.
8. ,, small do. do.
9. ,, long grove in rear end.
10. ,, short do. do.
11. ,, extraction cam on lever.
12. ,, recess in lever for locking bolt.
13. ,, lightening hole in knob of lever.
14. Striker, front collar.
15. ,, flats.
16. ,, collars for cocking-piece.
17. Bolt plug, screw thread.
18. Cocking-piece, cylindrical portion.
19. Cocking-piece, tooth.
20. ,, ,, bent.
21. ,, ,, recess for safety catch.
22. ,, stripping nib.
23. Extractor, claw.
24. ,, nib.
25. ,, recess for lugs of ring.
26. ,, tail.
27. Body, hood.
28. ,, rib.
29. ,, lugs for sear.
30. ,, housing for locking bolt.
31. Body, recess for bolt lever.
32. ,, backsight bed.
33. ,, wings for protecting backsight.
34. ,, charger guides.
35. ,, extraction cam.
36. ,, tang.
37. Ring, retaining handguard.
38. Sear, safety stud.
39. ,, lugs.
40. ,, nose.
41. ,, spring.
42. Trigger, first point on head.
43. ,, second do.
44. Locking bolt, plunger.
45. ,, ,, groove.
46. Safety catch, thumb-piece.
47. ,, ,, eccentric stem.
48. ,, ,, half moon.
49. Bolt stop, thumb-piece.
50. ,, ,, stop block.
51. Ejector.
52. Backsight, spring.
53. ,, fixed sight aperture.
54. ,, stop screw.
55. ,, aperture.
56. ,, slide catch.
57. Magazine, bottom plate.
58. ,, catch.
59. ,, undercut rib of bottom plate.
60. ,, spring.
61. ,, platform.
62. Trigger guard, front screw.
63. ,, ,, back screw.

TOOLS REQUIRED FOR STRIPPING OR ASSEMBLING RIFLES, MAGAZINE, ·303-INCH P/14.

Name.	No.	Use.
Vice	1	Fixing rifle.
Clams, armourers, standing vice.	1	To prevent damage to rifle.
Corks, clam ...	2	To prevent damage to fittings.
Horses, armourers ...	2	Support rifle.
Screwdrivers :— Armourers, small ...	1	(a) Screws, swivel. (b) Screw, nosecap. (c) Screw disc, marking butt.
Armourers, large ...	1	(a) Screws, guard trigger. (b) Screw strap, butt plate. (c) Screw spring trap, butt plate. (d) Screws, bracket, swivel butt. (e) Screw fixing dial sight. (f) Bolt tie fore-end. (g) To lightly jamb locking bolt.
Extractor Axis, M.L.M.	1	(a) Screw axis, stop bolt. (b) Screw axis, back sight. (c) Screw spring, back sight. (d) Screw stop, slide back sight.
Forked dial sight, M.L.M.	1	(a) Screw sight dial pivot.
Pincers, armourers	1	Removing screws that stick after unscrewing.
Mallets, rawhide	1	Removing or replacing nosecap.
Hammers, rivetting, 4 oz. ...	1	General.
Dummy cartridge, Mark VII	1	Removing plate magazine.

Drifts :—
    Magazine catch pin, M.L.M.
	1	Removing :—
		    (a) Pin axis sear.
		    (b) Pin axis, trigger.
		 Driving all pins flush.

Sight axis pin, M.L.M....	1	(a) Pin axis catch magazine. (b) Pin axis trap, butt plate. (c) Pin stop band, lower.
Wire, small ...	1	(a) Pin tie stock. (b) Pin fixing, block band f.s. To facilitate compressing spring bolt locking.

Name.	No.	Use.
Pin, fixing, stud, head catch slide, b.s., R.S.M.L.E.	1	Pin axis, catch slide b.s.
Metal	1	Removing or replacing plate cover locking bolt.
Centre punch	1	(Only when necessary) for fixing foresight, also for fixing certain screws.
Implement action, R.M. ·303-inch, P/14	1	General.
Braces, armourers'	1	With bits, screwdriver.
Bits, screwdriver:— Butt plate screw	1	
Tool stripping bolt, No. 2, Mark I.	1	
Tools, adjusting, f.s., R.M., ·303-inch, P/14, Cramp.	1	(Only when necessary.)

Tools and appurtenances required for cleaning, clearing, &c. (see page 8).

ADDITIONAL TOOLS, &C., REQUIRED FOR EXAMINING THIS RIFLE.

Name.	No.	Use.
Testers, trigger pull	1	Weighing springs.
Reflectors, mirror, S.A. ·303-in.	1	Examining bore.
Reflectors, mirror, S.A. ·303-in. adapters.	1	
Gauge, armourers', striker, point, R.M. ·303-inch, P/14	1	Protusion from ·05-in.–·055-in., radius ·03-in.
Gauges, plugs. (See page 7.)	5	(See page 53.)
Cartridges, S.A., dummy, ·303-in. inspectors—Mark IV.	5	Testing the feed.
Charges, ·303-in.	1	
Cases, cartridge, ·303-in. (fired).	1	Testing primary extraction and ejection.

STRIPPING AND ASSEMBLING.

Rifle, Magazine, ·303 in., pattern 1914.

To facilitate stripping or assembling, the rifle should be fixed in position in accordance with these instructions and illustrations.

Components should be removed or replaced strictly in the order tabulated.

1ST POSITION.

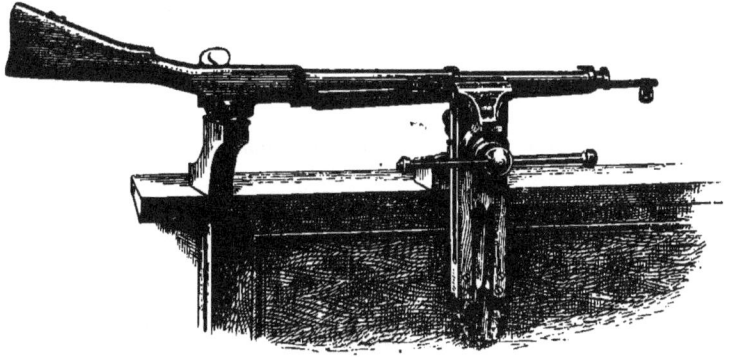

Supported on the *left horse* immediately in front of the *wings* on the bed backsight, and clamped at the *band lower* clear of the handguard rear.

Stripping.

Remove.	Detail.
‡ Screw, swivel, and swivel, piling.	
Screw, nose cap.	
‡ Screw, swivel, and swivel band.	
† Nose cap.	With mallet rawhide, tap off clear of stock.
* Plate, bottom magazine with spring and platform.	With the point of a bullet depress the catch and slide the plate to the rear.
Screws, guard trigger, front and back ...	Unscrew alternately.
Guard, trigger, with catch and spring, plate magazine.	Grip front between thumb and finger of right hand to ensure it being lifted horizontally.
§ Case, magazine.	
Handguard, front ...	Grasp the rifle in rear of the dial sight and unclamp the vice.

Remove.	Detail.
Band, lower ...	Spring open with thumb to clear pin stop and slide to the front clear of the stock.
Handguard, rear	Grasp rifle in front of position for lower band. Ease guard to the front.
Stock ...	Retain the grip with right hand and support the body with the left; separate the body with barrel from the stock by lightly tapping the heel of the butt on the shoulder of the left horse, easing grip with right hand as the parts separate. N.B.—Allow body to depress first, to prevent damage to sharp corners on stock.

FITTING THE ACTION AND BARREL TO STOCK.

Supported on the *left horse* and clamped at the parallel portion of the butt.

Slide the nose cap and lower band to the front end and the ring, retaining, to the rear end.

Take up the action, etc., holding the front end of barrel in rear of nose cap and band, between the thumb and finger of left hand, and grip the body at the bed, backsight, between the thumb and fingers of right hand.

Rest the front end of barrel in its groove in stock, and adjust the ring, retaining, to fit correctly into its recess (*a*), carefully lower the action into the stock, taking care that the screw, stop bolt, enters the hole (*b*) prepared to receive it.

Assembling.

Replace.	Detail.
Handguard, rear ...	Place in position, slightly raising the front end to facilitate the entry of rear end under the flange of the ring, retaining.
Band, lower.	
Handguard, front.	
† Nose-cap	Grip tightly round the front end of handguard and stock to facilitate fitting on.

FIX THE RIFLE IN THE 1ST POSITION (Page 43).

Assembling.

In reverse order.

Note.—
* Place in position, with end of plate touching trigger guard, press down flush and slide forward to engage.
† Great care to prevent damage to front end of handguard.
‡ Short end of swivels should be on the near side.
§ Care should be taken to ensure that the projecting portion of the guide plate enters its recess in the body. When fitted correctly the guide plate is flush with the bottom of the cartridge lead.

2ND POSITION.

Clamped firmly in front of the reinforce.

Stripping.

Remove.	Detail.
Bolt breech	Turn the safety catch to the front. Raise bolt lever to its full extent. Pull the stop bolt clear and draw bolt out.

46

Remove.	Detail.
‡ Screw, axis bolt stop.	Raise sight aperture. Press against rear end of stop bolt to take the weight of spring; while using drivers screw extractor axis to give screw about 5 complete turns and lift out.
† Stop bolt, with spring and ejector.	
Sight aperture.	
Plate, cover, locking bolt.	Use metal drift, tap down lightly to clear dovetail.*
Catch, safety, and bolt locking with spring.	Turn safety catch to 6˙ o'clock. Insert drift wire small into bolt chamber underneath the flat on stem of safety catch and press the bolt forward. Retain the bolt in this position by lightly wedging the blade of a large screwdriver between the side of the locking bolt and the body to retain spring in a state of compression. (N.B.—Use only sufficient force to just jamb the bolt.) Draw the catch clear. Place the drift against the head of bolt, remove screwdriver and ease spring down Insert drift and press out bolt with spring to the rear.
Pin, axis sear, and sear with spring and trigger.	Easing tension of spring press out to the left with a drift.

(Only to be removed for special instruction or repair.)

Backsight:—

* Nut and screw axis, b.s.	Hold nut while unscrewing axis; when clear take the weight of spring and remove.
Screw spring, b.s.	
Spring, b.s.	Ease to the front to clear dovetail.

Assembling.

In reverse order.

Note.—
* Use a pilot pin to facilitate replacing of axis screw.
† That the ejector is in its most forward position in the stop bolt.
‡ The rear end of stop bolt must be pressed in and retained to prevent stripping the threads.
§ Depress the platform magazine to give clearance for the bolt.

---

* The plate, cover, locking bolt, may be held by a fixing screw.

STRIPPING AND ASSEMBLING COMPONENTS.
Rifle, Magazine, ·303-inch, P/1914.

Stock.

Supported on the left horse and clamped just in rear of the grip.

Stripping.

Remove.	Detail.
Sight dial:—	
Screw pivot...	Use driver, screw, fork dial sight.
* Spring.	
Pointer.	
Screw fixing	Unscrew three complete turns. Then tap lightly on head of screw to loosen dial plate, complete unscrewing and remove.
Plate.	
Plate butt:—	
Screw, strap	Use large screwdriver.
Screw, plate butt and plate.	Use brace with bit.

Clamped in rear of grip toe uppermost.

Bracket, swivel, butt.	Use large screwdriver.

Assembling.

In reverse order.

Note.—Washer screw fixing dial sight is in position.
  * Concave face outwards.
  Collars, screw, guard, trigger are in position.

Trigger Guard.

Stripping.

Remove.	Detail.
Case, magazine ...	Press out from underside of guard.
Pin, axis catch, catch, magazine, and spring.	Fix the guard in vice. Use drift (cylindrical pin).

Assembling.

In reverse order.

Plate, Spring and Platform Magazine.

Dismantling.

Separate.	Detail.
Spring and plate	Raise the bend of spring and draw the blade from undercut grooves in plate.
*Spring and platform	Raise the bend of spring and draw the blade from the undercut grooves in platform.

Assembling.
Reverse the motions.

Note.—
* The narrow end of spring fits in the platform.

STOP BOLT.
Stripping.

Remove.	Detail.
Spring stop bolt and ejector	Press the ejector to the rear as far as possible, then press down on the toe of ejector to disengage the nibs of spring.

Assembling.

Place ejector in position as shown in sketch, with its curve form resting on the back of stop bolt, and the heel just fouling on the wall in front of slot and retain by gentle side pressure on the ejector.

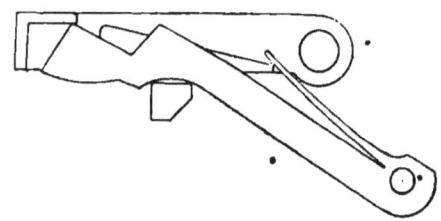

Keeping the tail of bolt spring down, engage the nibs, and press the ejector to the front.

SEAR.
Stripping.

Remove.	Detail.
Pin, axis, trigger, and trigger	Use drift (cylindrical pin).

Assembling.
In reverse order.

LEAF BACKSIGHT.
Stripping.

Remove.	Detail.
Screw, stop slide.	
Slide backsight... ...	Disengage the catch from rack on side of leaf and draw off.
Pin, axis, catch slide and spring	(Repair only.)

Assembling.
In reverse order.

BUTT PLATE.
Stripping.

Remove.	Detail.
Trap butt plate:—	
Screw and *spring	Use large screwdriver.
Pin axis	Use drift sight axis pin M.L.M.

Assembling.

Note.—
* Concave form uppermost.

BOLT BREECH.
Stripping.

Remove.	Detail.
† Extractor	Revolve counter clockwise to clear nib from cannelure, then press off to the front.
* Bolt plug with cocking piece, striker, and main spring.	Place the slot in the stripping tool over the bent (20) on the cocking piece, and pull the latter to the rear until the ears of the tool can be engaged over the cylindrical part of the cocking piece behind the bolt plug. Unscrew, turning to the left.
Cocking piece from striker.	Grip the bolt plug in the vice with its slot uppermost and the rear end just clear of the left side of the clams. Press the striker back as far as possible, remove tool; then turn the cocking piece through $\frac{1}{4}$-circle to disengage the interrupted collars and draw off.
Striker and main spring from bolt plug.	Ease up the striker and allow the mainspring to expand.

Assembling.
In reverse order.

Note.—There are flats on the striker corresponding to those in the bolt plug and cocking piece.
  * Screw the plug into the bolt as far as possible, then turn back to bring the toe of cocking piece opposite the notch (10) in the bolt. Disengage the ears of the tool, and ease the cocking piece forward, allowing the tooth (19) to enter the notch (10).
  † Press on the ring to bring the lugs (6) together.

ACTION OF THE MECHANISM R.M. '303-IN. P/14.

Assume the magazine to be charged and a cartridge just fired.

Raising the bolt lever.—The bolt is revolved, but the grooves in the body prevent the cocking piece and extractor from turning, and the bolt plug is held by its shoulder (17a) coming in contact with the bolt bed.

The actions resulting from the rotation of the bolt may be considered in the following stages :—

As the bolt commences to revolve, the cam-shaped wall of the long slot (9) in the bolt bears against the tooth (19) of the cocking piece and forces the latter to the rear, thus withdrawing the striker point into the face of the bolt and slightly compressing the mainspring.

In the next stage, the bolt lever clears the recess (31) in body, and the tooth (19), riding on the rear end of the bolt, retains the striker in the withdrawn position.

As the movement is continued, the primary-extraction cam (11) on the bolt lever, rides on the face (35), forcing the bolt slightly to the rear and thus unseating the cartridge case.

During the final stage of the movement, the retaining notch (10) in the bolt is brought opposite the tooth (19) on the cocking piece, and the tooth is forced into engagement by the action of the mainspring.

At the end of the movement, the bolt is arrested by the shoulder (11a) on the bolt lever coming in contact with the sight bed. In this position, the cocking piece and bolt plug are locked to the bolt, being thus retained in the correct position when closing the latter; the flats (7) on the bolt are over the safety stud (88), so permitting the sear to trip over the cocking piece on the backward movement of the bolt; the lugs (3, 4) are clear of the seating cams in the hood (27) and opposite their guide grooves in the bolt way; the rim of cartridge case is in the guide groove on the bolt face (1) and is held by the claw (28) of the extractor.

The bolt is now in the unlocked position ready to be withdrawn.

Drawing back the bolt.—As the bolt is withdrawn, the lugs (3, 4) enter their guide grooves in the bolt-way and prevent the bolt turning when in the withdrawn position; the sear (40) trips over the cocking piece; the cartridge case being held by the extractor is withdrawn with the bolt, and is released towards the end of the movement by the ejector (51), which enters the slot in the lug (4) and engages the base of the case. This causes the case to tilt about the claw (28) of the extractor and fly out to the right; the magazine is uncovered and as soon as the face (1) of the bolt clears the rim of the top cartridge, the latter rises slightly and is held against the magazine lip with its base partly projecting into the bolt-way. (The latter action takes place just prior to the ejection of the fired case.)

The backward travel of the bolt is arrested by the left lug (4) coming in contact with the stop bolt (50).

Pushing forward the bolt.—As the bolt moves forward, the ejector (51) is pressed back into its retracted position; the lower part of the bolt face (1) engages the base of the cartridge, forcing the latter forward, causing its front end to ride up the lead and the rim to move along its guide until it leaves the magazine lip, when the rear end of the cartridge jumps up under the influence of the spring (60) and the rim enters the guide on the bolt face (1) behind the claw (23) of the extractor. The cartridge is finally centred on the bolt face, as it moves forward in the chamber; the bent (20) of the cocking piece comes in contact with the nose (40) of the sear, thus retaining the cocking piece with striker, while the bolt with bolt plug moves forward, compressing the main spring.

This movement is stopped by the extraction cam (11) coming against the face (35) under the sight bed.

Turning down the bolt lever.—The inclined face of the locking lugs (3, 4) bear against the seating cams in the hood (27) and force the bolt forward, thereby (a) fully compressing the main spring (b) seating the cartridge firmly in the chamber and (c) providing a rigid support for the bolt on firing.

As the bolt lever reaches the end of its movement, the clearance groove (8) and the long slot (9) in the bolt, are brought opposite the safety stud (38) on the sear and the tooth (19) on the cocking piece respectively. The movement is arrested by the stop (12a) on the bolt lever coming in contact with the bottom of its recess (31) in the body.

COCKED POSITION.

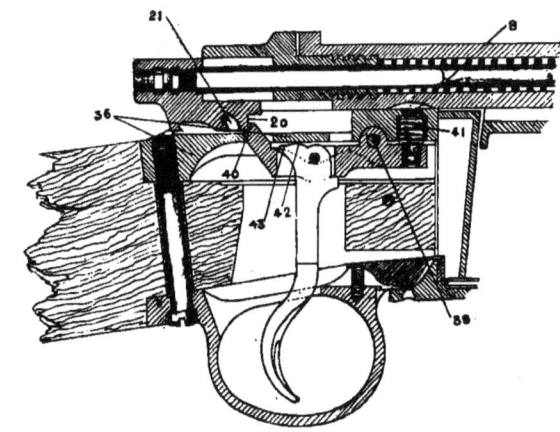

Pulling the trigger.—There are two distinct movements of the trigger, commonly termed the 1st and 2nd pulls, respectively. The former acts about the forward portion of the cam face (42)

and gives a greater mechanical advantage than the latter, which acts about its point (43).

1st Pull.—The cam face (42) bearing against the tang (36), causes the sear to rock on its axis (39) compressing the spring (41), and the safety stud (38) entering the clearance groove (8) allows the nose (40) to slide down to near the bottom of the bent (20) on the cocking piece.

2nd Pull.—The point of the cam face (43) is brought into play and the nose (40) being further depressed, disengages the bent (20), the cocking piece thus released is propelled forward by the main spring, the striker point passes through the hole in the bolt face and hits the cap of the cartridge.

When the finger piece of the trigger is released, the spring (41) reasserts itself and returns the trigger and sear to their normal positions.

Safety Devices.

1. *To prevent the cartridge being fired before the bolt reaches the locked position.*—As the safety stud (38) is prevented from rising by the cylindrical portion of the bolt, the nose (40) cannot be depressed and the cocking piece released until the bolt reaches the locked position, when the clearance groove (8) is brought over the stud (38).

2. *To obviate any tendency of the bolt to turn during firing.*—The safety stud (38) engages in the groove (8) on the bolt.

3. *To prevent the rifle being fired accidentally.*—The safety catch (46) is turned to the rear causing the half moon (48) to rise up into the recess (21) and lock the cocking piece; this locking action forces the cocking piece slightly to the rear, a movement not necessary for locking purposes, but essential as a further safety device. Otherwise, by reasons of clearance due to wear of the parts (48, 21), or fingering the trigger, the nose (40) might be underneath the bent (20), and thus result in the cartridge being prematurely fired when the safety catch is turned to the front again.

To Secure the Bolt in the Rifle.

The safety catch is turned to the rear, and its eccentric stem (47) bearing against the head of the locking bolt plunger (44), forces the latter to enter the recess (12) in the bolt lever.

To Prevent Snapping.

When the magazine is empty the platform (61) rises and its rib arrests the forward travel of the bolt.

NOTE.—A Depressor platform is issued for drill purposes.

TESTING BORE OF BARRELS FOR WEAR.

Before applying the gauges, see that the barrel is thoroughly cleaned and free from metallic fouling, bulges, cuts, or bends. The ·303" plug should then run through the bore. The barrels are sentenced as unserviceable if—(1) ·307" plug runs through, or (2) ·308" plug enters muzzle ·25" (*i.e.*, to line on plug), or (3) ·310" plug enters breech ;25", or (4) the No. 2 lead plug enters breech ·5".

The ·310" and lead plugs are required to pass into the breech end of the barrel until their ends are flush with (or below) the breech face of the barrel before the amount of wear allowed is recorded. The distance lines on these plugs, when flush with the breech face of the barrel, are to show that the front end of the plug has arrived at the position in the bore, or lead, in which the plug commences to record breech wear. In the case of M.M. and M.E. arms the bottom of the cartridge head recess represents the breech race of barrel.

(N.B. In a barrel in which the lead is but slightly worn, it will not be possible for the ·310" plug to enter so that the line on its rear end flushes with the breech face of the barrel. This will be due to the fact that the front portion of the lead from chamber to bore has not been enlarged by wear to the diameter of the plug.)

Reference gauges are kept at A.O.D. stations to periodically check those used by armourers by comparison with the reference gauges in worn barrels, etc. The reference gauges are stamped " REFERENCE," in addition to the usual marking.

Sentencing Cord-Worn Barrels. (*See* Appendix XXV, R.A.O.S.)

To determine the serviceability of a cord-worn barrel, the following points should be observed :—

(*a*) A barrel will be considered unserviceable through cord wear at breech end when the *fired case* shows clear signs of having *expanded into the cord groove.*

(*b*) If the wear exists at the muzzle, barrels should, if possible, be practically tested for accuracy, as laid down in M.R., 1909 (Reprint 1912). If a 500 yards range is not available, the rifle should be fired at 100 feet range, when the centres of the best 9 out of 10 shots should fall within a circle 1·75 inches in diameter.

Note.—Cord wear in barrels is caused by the pull-through cord rubbing against the breech or muzzle end of the barrel when the pull-through is not drawn through the barrel in line with the bore. The friction ultimately cuts a groove which may lead to burst cases when it occurs at the breech end, and destroys accuracy when it occurs at the muzzle.

Explanation of Various Marks on Rifles.

Mark.	Where Found.	Meaning.
E.Y.	Butt, fore-end, body, barrel and bolt.	May be utilized in case of emergency.
D.P.	Ditto	For drill purposes.
M.T.	Ditto	For use with ·23-inch Morris tube.
A.T.	Ditto	For use with ·22-inch aiming tube and ·22-inch rim-fire cartridge.
	Marks on Barrel.	
Year of manufacture.	Underneath Knox form.	
Rotation number and series letter.	On right of Knox form.	
P.	Left of Knox form ...	Parallel bore.
✱	Front of Knox form ...	Rust or cut inside barrel.
✱	On other positions of the barrel.	Corrosion or rust on exterior of barrel near the star.
✱W.	Left side of Knox form, at front end of reinforce for muzzle, and rear end for breech.	Cord-worn. Inspection Department marking.
R. ...	Knox form ... ✱ ...	Found rusty by examiner and to be cleaned by armourer.
(✱) ...	Same as ✱	If marked by A.O.D., to distinguish from Inspection Department marking.
(Ẇ) ...	Same as ✱W.	Cord-worn. A.O.D. marking.
H.V. ...	Barrel, rifles, short, behind backsight; rifles, charger loading, in front of backsight.	Suitable for Mark VII ammunition.

Also various proof and manufacturing marks will be found on the barrel.

Marks on body.

Manufacturer's initials and place of manufacture
Mark of rifle
Year of manufacture
} On right side, close to the stock butt. In converted rifles on the left side.

Rotation number and series letter. } On right side, close to the barrel.

Various proof and inspection marks.

Marks on other components.

Mark.	Where Found.	Meaning.
Rotation number and series letter.	Bolt, fore-end, nose-cap, and sight-leaf.	
S....	Fore-end	Early patterns of short rifles. Fitted with spring and stud.
2 ...	Right of butt ...	Early patterns. Plate keeper stock bolt in fore-end.
P....	Right of butt ...	Early patterns. Compressed butt.
S....	On stock-butt ...	Short butt, 12 inches.
L....	On stock-butt ...	Long butt, 13 inches.
L.E.S. 2 ...	On dial plate ...	Suitable for Mark VII ammunition.
2 ...	On slide backsight	Do.
3 ...	On magazine case	Do.
2 ...	On magazine platform	Do.
3 ...	On magazine auxiliary spring	Do.
4 ...	On magazine case ...	Do.
3 ...	On magazine platform	Do.
2 ...	On platform spring ...	Do.
4 ...	On magazine auxiliary spring	Do.
C.L.	At right bottom corner of sight-leaf.	Suitable for rifles C.L., M.L.E. Mark I sighted for Mark VII ammunition.
1*, 2	At right bottom corner of sight-leaf.	Suitable for rifles C.L. M.L.E. Mark I* sighted for Mark VII ammunition.
C.L.	On dial plate ...	Suitable for rifles C.L., M.L.E. Mark I and I* sighted for Mark VII ammunition.

Note.—The No. 4 magazine case and fittings are original manufacture. The No. 3 magazine case and fittings are conversions from Nos. 1 or 2 magazines.

The original slide backsight on Marks I, I*, I***, II, II* R.S.M.L.E. on being adapted for Mark VII ammunition was reversed, altered, and numbered 2. By reversing it, therefore, it again becomes suitable for rifles sighted for Mark VI ammunition.

SWORD BAYONETS.

There are six patterns of sword bayonets in use with magazine arms, viz.:—

    Pattern 1888. Marks I, II, and III. For long rifles.
       ,,   1903. Mark I.   ,, short ,,
       ,,   1907.   ,,   ,, ,, ,,
       ,,   1913.   ,,   ,, Rifle magazine, ·303-inch, P/14.

The various marks of the 1888 pattern differ only in small details.

The 1903 pattern differs from the 1888 pattern in having the ring of the cross-piece and the mortice on the same side. It has a larger nut and stronger bolt.

The 1907 pattern differs from previous patterns in having the blade five inches longer and single edged, with lightening grooves to bring it down to about the same weight as previous patterns. One end of the cross-piece is hooked. (Hook abolished October, 1913.)

The approximate weight of the above sword-bayonets is 16½ ozs.

The scabbards of 1888 and 1903 patterns are interchangeable for patterns 1888 and 1903 sword-bayonets. The 1907 scabbard is interchangeable with the 1913 sword bayonet.

Various Marks on Bayonets.

Mark.	Where found.	Meaning.
*	Pommel ...	Pommel blemished.
×	Blade ...	Convex side of blade for future bending.

WEBLEY PISTOL.

Six patterns may be met with in the service, viz. :—Marks I, I*, II, III, IV, V and VI. Some of the latter Marks and the Mark VI are provided with 6-inch barrels for the use of officers and cadets.

The Webley pistol was introduced in August, 1890, to supersede the Enfield pattern. It consists of (i) the barrel, (ii) the body, (iii) the cylinder.

The barrel is connected to the body by a knuckle joint and strap with spring lock. The body is slotted out to form seatings and bearings for the various parts of the breech action, and is provided with vulcanite grips in place of the wooden grips of the Enfield pistols. The cylinder has chambers for six cartridges, and is pivoted on a tubular axis attached to the barrel. The extractor works in this axis, surrounded by a spiral spring, and is actuated by a lever carried in the knuckle joint.

Calibre, ·441 inch.
Weight, 2 lbs. 3 ozs. to 2 lbs. 6½ ozs. approx.
Rifling, 7 grooves, 1 turn in 20 calibres, right-handed.
Muzzle velocity, 715 f.s. approx.
Sighted up to 50 yards.

Various Marks on Pistols.

Registered No.—On barrel, body, and cylinder.
Maker and Pattern.—On body and strap.
Date of Issue.—On body.
* On left side of the strap denotes cut or rust in bore.

STRIPPING AND ASSEMBLING.
Webley Pistols, Marks III, IV, V and VI.

Tools required :—Driver, screw, Extractor, axis, Pincers, armourers, and cramps.

Stripping.

Remove.	Detail.
Screw, stock.	
Stocks, left and right.	
Screws, guard, trigger, and guard.	
Spring, main	Ease stud out of seating, being careful to prevent the spring flying out. Cock the hammer. Pass the fork of cramp over the spring. Release the hammer. Take hold of cramp and disconnect spring from swivel hammer.
Spring, main, auxiliary.	Lift out of seating.
* Screw, trigger.	
Trigger, with pawl, cylinder catch, and spring	After removing, lift pawl off its pivot. Lift cylinder catch off its pivot, and, if necessary, remove screw spring cylinder catch and spring.
Screw, hammer.	
Hammer, with catch and swivel	After removing hammer, remove screw, swivel hammer, and swivel; also screw, catch hammer, and catch with spring.
Screw, fixing lever ...	Use suitable coin. Release barrel catch, and open the pistol to the fullest extent.
Cylinder, with extractor and spring	Press lever upwards until it causes cam to revolve slightly, and release cylinder, which can then be withdrawn. Unscrew nut extractor, and lift out spring and extractor.
Screw, lever, cam.	
* Lever, cam	Lift off its pivot.
Screw, joint axis.	
Pin, joint axis	Tap out towards the left.
Barrel	From body.
Extractor, lever, with auxiliary lever, spring, and pin	Ease out of seating in barrel.
Screws, cam cylinder and cam.	

Stripping—contd.

Remove.	Detail.
Screw, catch, barrel and catch	Press on thumb-piece and slip cramp over spring, thus removing the pressure off the catch.
Spring, catch, barrel ...	Ease off cramp and lift stud on spring out of its seating.
Shield	Special instruction and repair only.

Assembling.

In reverse order.

Note.—
* That the cylinder catch projects beyond its recess.

Examination of Webley Pistol.

Tools, &c., Required :—
 Testers trigger pull, Mark II.
 Gauges, armourers.
  Pistol, Webley—
   Hammer projection and radius of point.
   Distance of cylinder from face of body ·052 inch rejecting.

Note.—
That there are no parts deficient.
That all screws are home and fast.
That all parts fit and work properly, special attention being directed to the following :—

Number of Pistol.—Should be the same on barrel, body, and cylinder.

Barrel.—Bore should be free from cuts, rust, excessive scoring, or other damage.

Cylinder.—Chamber should be free from cuts, rust, &c. With the trigger pressed cylinder should only have but a very slight rotary movement. In the loading position it should revolve freely.

Extractor.—That it is working freely. Extracts and ejects freely.

Ratchet Teeth.—Not damaged nor unduly worn.

Pawl.—That its lifting point is not damaged and the safety stud is in good condition.

Trigger.—That the cylinder stop and trigger nose are not damaged or unduly worn.

* *Cylinder Catch.*—That its bents are in good condition and that it is actuated properly by its spring, also that its recess in the body is correct.

Hammer.—That the hammer catch is not unduly worn and the bents are in good condition.

---

* Correct nomenclature is "trigger stop."

The Action.—Test to see that the safety arrangements are correct, also that the cartridge is properly fed up and the cap struck central.

Protrusion and Figure of Hammer Nose.—Test with gauge. Should be between ·044 and ·054 inch.

Space between Face of Body and Cylinder.—Test with gauge. This ·052 slip gauge should not enter between the body and cylinder at the top.

Weighing of Springs.

(1) *Pull-off.*—Clamp the pistol in a vice by its barrel, and full-cock, apply T.T.P. to trigger. To release hammer a power of 6 to 8 lbs. is required.

(2) *Trigger Action.*—With hammer in fired position the pull on trigger to raise the hammer to full-cock—12 to 15 lbs.

(3) *Mainspring.*—Keeping trigger firmly pressed by finger so that hammer face bears on pistol body, apply the T.T.P. to a loop of twine passed over the head of hammer, and pull in direction of axis of barrel; the weight to move it—$3\frac{3}{4}$ to $4\frac{1}{4}$ lbs.

(4) *Barrel Catch Spring.*—Apply the tags on T.T.P. to the front top of catch and pull horizontally to the rear. The weight should be from 4 to 6 lbs.

Miss-fires with Webley Pistols.

May be caused by the following:—
  (i) Short nose to hammer.
  (ii) Hammer striking cap high, low, to the right, or left.
  (iii) Weak mainspring.
  (iv) Barrel catch not quite home.

Note.—The above may be remedied:—
  (i) By filing away a little of the shoulder of the hammer or replace by spare part.
  (ii) May be caused by backward or forward movement of cylinder on its axis, or excessive rotary movement on the axis due to worn ratchet teeth or lifting point of pawl. Replace defective part.
  (iii) Replace by spare component.
  (iv) Examine spring and catch, see that the axis screw is not over-tight, or replace defective part by spare one.

Pistol, Webley.—Action of Mechanism.

Cocking by Hand.—On pulling the hammer to the rear, the top shoulder of hammer bent bearing on the underside of trigger nose, causes the trigger to revolve, depressing the front end, which carries the cylinder catch,* and raising the rear end, which carries the pawl and cylinder stop. The front end of cylinder catch, coming in contact with the front of the slot in which it works, is stopped and the further movement of the trigger causes

---

* For instructional purposes the term "cylinder catch" is used. The correct nomenclature is "trigger stop."

the spring of the catch which is attached to the trigger to ride up the catch until its front end trips on to the top of the upper bent and jerks the catch upwards into one of the recesses on cylinder, which has meanwhile been brought into position as follows:—

As the trigger is pulled the pawl rises and engaging one of the ratchet teeth on the extractor causes the cylinder to be revolved until it is checked by the cylinder stop. The cartridge is thus brought to the correct position for firing. The cylinder catch comes into operation as explained above and acts as an extra means of holding the cylinder in the correct firing position.

During these movements the front end of auxiliary spring, which is resting on the shoulder of the pawl, is being lifted, and the swivel hammer is being lowered, thus compressing the mainspring.

The above movements are continued until the trigger nose engages in the hammer bent, thus retaining the hammer in the cocked position.

To Fire.—On pulling the trigger its nose is disengaged from the hammer bent, allowing the hammer to fly forward under pressure of the mainspring, striking the cap, thus firing the charge.

Note.—Since the trigger is being held back, the hammer catch is enabled to pass downwards behind the trigger nose.

Rebound Action.—On releasing the trigger it is caused to revolve by the pressure of the mainspring through the medium of the auxiliary acting on the pawl and thus lowering the pawl and cylinder stop, the cylinder meanwhile being held by the cylinder catch, thereby ensuring that the pawl will engage the correct tooth on the head of extractor.

During the movement of the trigger the shoulder of the auxiliary, acting against the rebound arm of the hammer, causes the hammer to revolve slightly to the rear, drawing back the hammer nose clear of the cartridge.

These movements continue until the trigger nose, tripping clear of the hammer catch, comes in contact with the shoulder on top of hammer bent. The spring of the hammer catch being free, forces the catch over the top of the trigger nose.

Trigger Action.—Pulling on the trigger causes it to revolve, thus raising pawl and cylinder stop and lowering cylinder catch. The top of the trigger nose bearing against the hammer catch causes the hammer to revolve to the rear and the mainspring to be compressed.

These movements continue until the cartridge is in position for firing, when the trigger nose, tripping clear of the hammer catch, allows the hammer to fall and fire the cap.

Safety Arrangements.—Owing to the slight working clearance between the various components, any forward pressure on the hammer causes it to revolve slightly to the front, thus lowering the hammer catch. At the same time, owing to the rebound arm of the hammer acting against the shoulder of auxiliary, the front end of auxiliary is lifted and, coming in contact with the safety stud on pawl, lifts the pawl and thereby slightly raises rear end of trigger, bringing the top of its nose into contact with the hammer catch, and thus locking the forward movement of the hammer and preventing it from coming in contact with the cartridge.

Note.—There is a slight movement of the trigger just prior to the pawl being lifted, due to the pressure exerted by the spring of the cylinder catch.

Ejection.—As the pistol is opened the shoulder of the body at the joint engaging bent on extractor lever causes the latter to revolve about its pivot the joint axis pin. The arm of the extractor therefore presses against and raises the " nut extractor " and " extractor " ejecting the empty cases.

As the extractor lever revolves its cam-shaped edge riding against the shoulder of the barrel at the joint causes the extractor lever, which has an elongated pivot hole, to move inwards until just after ejection its bent trips clear of the shoulder on the body and the spring of the nut extractor returns the extractor to its seating and the lever to its normal position.

On closing the pistol, the auxiliary lever acted upon by its spring pushes the extractor lever outwards and its bent is again positioned to engage the shoulder on the body.

Pistol, Smith & Wesson.—·455-inch, with 6½-inch barrel, Mark I, II.

Pistol, Colt.—·455-inch, with 5½-inch barrel, Mark I.

A number of these pistols have been issued to the Service.

They are designed to fire the ordinary service ammunition as issued for the Webley pistol.

The special ammunition issued for use with automatic pistols must not be used.

Instructions for Cleaning, and Clearing Jammed Pull-through or Flannelette from, Barrels of ·303-inch Rifles by Armourers.

(Instructions for cleaning by the soldier are given in the Musketry Regulations.)

(1) *N.B.*—The oil used must be " oil, G.S." No other lubricant is to be used for the bore of barrels, except that and paraffin mixed when cleaning with brass wire and jute and emery, as detailed below.

(2) *To clean a rusty barrel with the double pull-through.*—All barrels which are slightly rusty inside will be thoroughly cleaned by the armourer. A double pull-through, having a hand loop at one end to enable it to be used with assistance, is supplied for this purpose. It will be used without flannelette (the gauze being expanded as described hereunder) in the following manner:—

Remove the bolt; well oil the gauze of the pull-through, drop the weight through the barrel from the breech, clamp the muzzle guide on the muzzle of the barrel to prevent damage by friction of the cord, and pull the gauze to and fro until the rust is removed; care being taken to draw the pull-through out of the barrel in line with the bore, as any friction of the pull-through cord with the sides of the chamber at the breech causes the chamber to become oval, and thus renders the barrel unserviceable. When the gauze of the pull-through, in consequence of frequent use, ceases to fit the barrel tightly, narrow strips of flannelette or paper may be inserted under each side to increase its diameter.

(3) *To clean rusty barrels with brass wire, emery and jute.*—The eye of the rods Nos. 2 or 4 for wire will be filled with from 50 to 60 strands of brass wire, No. 26 S.W.G., hard, cut in 3-inch lengths, the ends will be pressed back along the length of the rod. The wire, being well oiled with a mixture of two volumes of " oil, G.S.," to one volume of paraffin oil, will be inserted in the muzzle end of the barrel, the arm, being held in a vice; the muzzle guide* will then be clamped on the muzzle and the rod worked up and down the bore to remove the rust.

In the case of short rifles the nose cap will have to be removed before using the muzzle guide.

If a barrel is very rusty it will be found easier to remove the rust if the muzzle of the barrel is plugged, and oil poured in from the breech end, and left to soak for a few hours.

After loosening the rust, wipe out the barrel with the rod, cleaning No. 1, for jute, and examine (the jute for this rod will be cut in about 8-inch lengths).

If a barrel is found to require further cleaning, coil the jute round so that it fits the bore tightly, and sprinkle on a little flour emery, replace in the barrel, and after clamping on the muzzle guide work the rod well up and down until the barrel is clean.

The rust being removed, a slightly pitted surface will usually remain; this should be greased with " oil, G.S."

To preserve the wire when the rods are not in use a cartridge case cut short at the shoulder will be found useful as a cap.

Rods, cleaning, for wire, are supplied in two lengths, No. 2 for long rifles, and No. 4 for short rifles, arranged so that the wire cannot pass beyond the front end of the chamber, owing to the difficulty of withdrawing it if it does so.

Rod, cleaning, No. 2, if fitted with the " Bush, stop, rod, cleaning, No. 2," is suitable for short rifles.

The rod, cleaning, No. 1 for jute is suitable for long or short rifles.

(4) *To Clean the Chamber.*—Fix the rifle in the vice and remove the bolt.

Insert the long edge of a piece of gauze wire in the slot of the stick. Fold the gauze round to the left, and finally close in the portion which overhangs the front of the stick.

---

* When a muzzle guide becomes worn in the cleaning rod guide hole, particular notice should be taken that there is no friction between the cleaning rod and the bore of the barrel, which is liable to render the barre. unserviceable.

Smear the gauze with oil, and insert the stick into the chamber.

Using the brace and bit, revolve the stick clockwise until the chamber is clear.

Replace the gauze with a piece of flannelette, and complete the operation of cleaning the chamber.

N.B.—The bit, Mark I., which is only $7\frac{3}{4}''$ long, necessitates the removal of the stock butt.

(5) *To clear the barrel when pull-through becomes broken and jammed.*—Screw the "plug clearing plain" on the "rod tool clearing ·303-inch arms," and place it in the barrel at the end nearest the jammed flannelette; compress the flannelette and cord as much as possible, then withdraw the rod and plug, unscrew the plug and screw on the bush and bit, screw, pass into the barrel, at the end nearest the jammed flannelette, and turn, pressing firmly against the jammed material until a firm grip is felt; then pull strongly on the rod, keeping the screw screwed tightly in the material by turning the rod whilst pulling.

NOTE.—No rod of soft metal or wood is ever to be used by armourers in cleaning or clearing the bore of barrels of ·303-inch arms; only the rods issued, which are of hard steel, should be used.

Clearing the Envelope of a Bullet or a Cartridge Case.

Screw the plug clearing plain on the tools clearing rod No. 2. Insert the plug into the muzzle end of the rifle, and force out the obstruction to the rear.

MAXIM GUNS IN THE SERVICE.

Gun, Maxim, ·45-in.—Martini-Henry Chamber.
Introduced into L.S. January, 1891.

Gun, Maxim, ·303-in.—Magazine Rifle Chamber.
Introduced into L.S. July, 1893.

Gun, Maxim, ·303-in. Converted Mk. I.—February, 1899.
(Converted from ·45-in. Maxim guns.)

Gun, Maxim, ·303-in. Converted Mk. II.—February, 1902.

The ·45-in. gun will only be met with in the Colonies, India and Egypt.

    The average weight for all = 60 lbs.
    The normal rate of fire = 450 rds. per min.
    With Mk. VII ammunition = 500 rds. per min.
    Water in barrel casing boils at 600 rds. with rapid fire.
      ,,   ,,   ,, evaporates 1¼ pints for each 1000 rds. if firing continuous.
    ·45-in. Sighted up to about 2000 yds.
    ·303-in. Converted ,, 2500 ,,
    ·303-in. Guns with Mk. VI ammunition 2900 yds.
    ·303-in. Guns with Mk. VII ammunition 2800 ,,

    The conversion of ·45-in. guns to ·303-in. converted Mark I consists in the substitution of ·303-in. barrels, and the altering of various components to suit the smaller calibre barrel. The latter is of the same external diameter as the ·45-in. barrel, and has a special muzzle attachment.

    The converted Mark II gun differs from last in being fitted with the Service ·303-in. barrel and attachment for ball firing.

    The action, stripping, &c., is identical, for all practical purposes, to that of the Service ·303-in. gun.

MUZZLE ATTACHMENT FOR BALL FIRING.

    Provided in order to increase the force of recoil. *Must always be used with Converted Guns.* Should be used with ·303-in. gun when, on account of a badly worn lead, dirt, dried oil, or the water freezing in the barrel casing, the recoil of the barrel is insufficient to work the gun after the usual remedies of adjusting the fusee spring and oiling the working parts have been tried.

    It is screwed into the packing gland seating at the front end of the barrel casing, the screwed end of the attachment acting as a packing gland.

·303-in. MAXIM MACHINE GUN.
Nomenclature of Parts of Gun.

Barrel	With asbestos packing; gunmetal valve.
Barrel casing ...	With ejector tube spring; steam tube with slide valve and keeper screw; packing gland; asbestos packing; two screwed plugs, each with chain, S hooks, and stud; nipple, cork plug with chain and S hooks; muzzle cover with chain and two S hooks.
Breech casing...	With buffer spring; check lever with collar and split pin; slides, right and left; trigger bar; fusee spring box.
Condenser, steam	Consisting of Mk. IV G.S. nose bag, with strap; 6 feet of ⅜-in. flexible metallic tubing, with female union.
Cover	With joint pin, collar and fixing pin; cover lock, with piston, spring and stop screw; ammunition label with four rivets; cover springs.
Crank	With crank pin and fixing pin; connecting rod; adjustable with cotter; crank handle and fixing pin; fusee with chain, spring and adjusting screw.
Feed block ...	With slide; top and bottom levers, with spring fixing pin; top and bottom pawls, with axis pin; slide springs; feed block spring; band roller with axis pin, collar and fixing pin.
Lock	Consisting of casing with side levers and screwed head; extractor levers, right and left; extractor with spring and fixing pin; gib with gib spring and cover; extractor stop with keeper and fixing pins; sear with spring and axis pin; trigger with axis and fixing pins; tumbler with axis and fixing pins; firing pin; lock spring, with axis and fixing pins; keeper bracket.
Rear cross-piece	With fixing pin; firing lever, with spring, axis and fixing pins; safety catch and axis pin; piston and spring; shutter with pivot screw; milled heads with leather washers and oil brushes.
Side plates ...	Side plate, right, with side plate spring; side plate, left, with connecting rod spring.
Sight, fore ...	With fixing screw.

Note.—Guns arranged to fire Mark VII ammunition are fitted with a No. 2 feed block and lock, and a graduated plate, Mark III, which is graduated up to 2,800 yards. The solid cams are altered in form. The feed blocks and locks are stamped with the figure "2," the former on the left side and the latter on the side and extractor levers. Guns so arranged are suitable for firing Mark VI ammunition also, it only being necessary to change the graduated plate.

(B 12813) C

Sight, tangent	Consisting of stem, graduated plate, and two fixing screws; slide with pinion, pawl and fixing pin; tangent sight slide spring; milled head and fixing screw; axis pin; tangent sight spring and piston.

Details Appertaining to Tools and Accessories used for Stripping, &c.

Nomenclature.	Use.
	Carried in Wallet.
Plug, clearing	Removing separated cartridge case from chamber.
Punches No. 2...	Driving out large axis and fixing pins, driving small pins flush, and driving home small pins
,, No. 3...	Driving out pin axis sear.
,, No. 4...	Driving out pins fixing, extractor spring and striker, firing pin. To act as a pilot pin, for pin, axis lock spring.
Balances, spring	Weighing springs and testing resistance offered to recoiling portion.
Pliers, cutting	Wiring axis pins.
Screwdriver, small.	Screw fixing, graduation plate and removing cover, gib spring.
Spanner, shifting	Removing or replacing fusee.
Key, gland and steam tube.	Screwing up or unscrewing packing gland and steam tube.
Pull-through, double.	Removing rust or metallic fouling from barrel.
	Carried in Case.
Protector, muzzle	To prevent cord wear at muzzle.
Reflector, mirror M.G.	To facilitate examining interior of barrel.
Funnel, filling...	To facilitate filling barrel casing.
	Carried in Box.
Bag, water and nozzle.	
Key, gib, gun-metal valve.	Screwing up or unscrewing valve.
Hammer ...	General service.
Screwdriver, bent.	General service.
Screwdriver, large.	Screws fixing, foresight, milled head, and crank handle. Screws, pivot shutter, keeper steam tube, and stop cover lock.
Tool, belt repairing.	Fixing eyelets and strips in belt.
Plugs, belt Maxim.	Opening out pockets in belt.

NOTE.—The Case, including Wallet, is part of the contents of the Box. It should always accompany the gun when in action, the Box being left in the wagon line.

Carried either in Gun Case or in Case, Spare Barrel and Cleaning Rod.

Rods, cleaning	Cleaning interior of barrel.

With Armourer's Tools.

Mallets, raw hide	For removal or replacement of rear cross-piece and breech casing.
Drifts (copper headed)	Driving large axis, fixing and joint pins flush, driving large pins home, also removing crank handles and ejector tube spring.

FOOTNOTE.—For complete details of:—
  Box, spare parts and tools,
    Maxim, ·303-in. Land (Marks I*, II*, III*, and IV),
see Paragraph 16738, List of Changes, April, 1914.

STRIPPING ·303-in. MAXIM.

The gun is stripped in the following order :—

Note.—All pins are driven in from R—L, and out *vice versa.*

(1) *Lock and Feed Block:*—Raise cover, turn crank handle on to buffer spring, see that extractor drops, place finger between extractor and stop, raise lock and allow crank handle to come slowly back on to check lever; slide live cartridges out of extractor. Give lock $\frac{1}{8}$ turn to the left and lift off. Lift feed block out.

(2) *Fuzee Spring Box:*—With right hand at the rear and left at front, press box forward until clear of lugs and remove. Disconnect fusee chain and remove box and spring. Care should be taken to throw no cross strain on the chain.

(3) *Tangent Sight and Cover Lock:*—Place a screwdriver across the breech casing, to bear underneath the gunmetal block and lower the cover. Drive out axis pin of stem and remove with its piston and spring. Close the cover, press in the cover lock with large screwdriver, remove stop screw; the lock with its piston and spring can then be removed.

(4) *Cover:*—Drive out fixing pin of cover joint pin, remove collar and joint pin, and take off cover.

(5) *Rear Cross-piece:*—Drive out tapered fixing pin, grasp with the left hand the left handle of the rear cross-piece, slightly raise the casing and, with mallet, strike top edges of casing alternately until rear cross-piece is clear of the dovetails on the casing. Lift out the trigger bar.

(6) *Slides (R. and L.) and Check Lever:*—Pull out the slides. Drive out fixing pin from check lever collar, remove collar and check lever.

(7) *Recoiling Portion:*—Fold back connecting rod on to crank, turn crank handle vertical and draw out to the rear the recoiling portion. Disconnect side plates by dropping them and springing them outwards. If necessary, by taking out the fixing pin, the crank handle can be driven off with a drift and hammer, and the fusee unscrewed from left bearing of crank, but as a rule these parts are not required to be stripped.

(8) *Foresight:*—First carefully mark its position then remove fixing screw and foresight.

(9) *Condenser.*—Unscrew union from nipple.

(10) *Steam Tube and Packing Gland.*—Up-end the barrel casing so that it stands on the rear end of the breech casing. Remove the keeper screw and unscrew the steam tube. Unscrew and remove the packing gland and packing.

(11) *Breech and Barrel Casings† and Ejector Tube Spring*.*—Rest the barrel casing on a table or bench, with the filling hole uppermost, and the breech casing clear of bench; place the left hand

under the breech casing and strike the top edges alternately with a mallet, and the casings will come apart. Lift the ejector tube spring with the point of the screwdriver and tap out the spring with the drift and hammer.

Note.—The breech and barrel casings should only be separated when repairs are necessary. Care must be taken not to strike the barrel casing, and the blows should be struck as close to the dovetailing as possible.

(12) *Lock.*—(1) Release lock spring and lay the lock on bench left side uppermost. Then drive out sear, tumbler, and lock spring axis pins. (2) Remove keeper bracket, lock spring, tumbler, firing pin, extractor levers, and sear. (3) Drive out trigger axis pin, extractor stop keeper pin, remove trigger, extractor stop, and slide extractor from face of lock casing. (4) Push out gib spring cover, take out gib spring and gib. (5) Drive out extractor spring fixing pin, and remove extractor spring.

(13) *Feed Block.*—(1) Drive out spring fixing pin of top and bottom levers, drive out bottom lever and remove top lever and slide. (2) Drive out axis pin of bottom pawls and remove pawls with feed block spring. (3) Drive out fixing pin of band roller axis pin, remove collar, axis pin and band roller. (4) Remove top pawls from slide by pressing them outwards. The springs for pawls if weak or broken are only to be removed by an armourer or qualified artificer.

(14) *Tangent Sight.*—(1) Remove the top fixing screw of graduated plate. (2) Remove fixing screw of the milled head, and lift the latter off the slide. (3) Run the slide off the stem. (4) Remove fixing pin, pawl and pinion from slide. (5) Remove bottom fixing screw of graduated plate and remove latter from the stem. (6) Place the milled head, face upwards, on a bench, then with a drift applied to the rectangular nib on "spring slide" knock the latter down flush with the face, when it can be lifted out with the pliers.

(15) *Rear Cross-piece.*—(1) Drive out axis pin of firing lever, and remove the latter with its spiral spring. (2) Drive out axis pin of safety catch, and lift out the latter, also the piston and spring from their seating. (3) Remove pivot screw and shutter. (4) Unscrew, from the handles, the milled heads with their leather washers, and oil brushes.

Before assembling the gun all parts should be tried in their places separately to see that they work freely.

ASSEMBLING ·303-in. MAXIM GUN.

Reverse all the foregoing operations with the exception that the recoiling portions must be replaced before the packing and gland (10).

Note:—

(14) (2)—Assemble the milled head with the arms of the slide spring outside the lugs on the pawl.

(13) (2)—Pawls and block are stamped F and R respectively to ensure longer pawl being placed at the front.

(11) *—Should be in position and weighed before joining the casings together.

(11) †—Casings should be turned upside down. They are correctly assembled when the bearings for the cross-head joint pin are aligned. When assembled the recoiling portions should be lubricated, worked backwards and forwards to ease the packing, distribute the lubricant, &c.

REPLACEMENT OF DEFECTIVE PARTS OF THE LOCK.

Should any of the components belonging to the lock become defective, they can be replaced from the spare parts, without stripping the lock right down. Proceed as follows:—

(1) *Sear.*—Fully cock, lift the sear, and *hang up* the firing pin with the tumbler and trigger; with the lock on a bench, left side up, drive out the sear axis pin, and remove the sear with its spring.

(2) *Tumbler.*—Fully cock, thus hanging up the firing pin on the sear; drive out the axis pin of tumbler, *pull the trigger slightly*, and lift out tumbler.

Note.—Care should be taken not to allow the screwed head to lift the sear once the tumbler has been removed.

(3) *Trigger, lock spring or extractor levers.*—Release the lock spring, drive out the lock spring axis pin, remove keeper bracket, extractor levers and lock spring; if the trigger is defective drive out the trigger axis pin and remove the trigger.

(4) *Firing Pin.*—Proceed as for (3) but do not remove the trigger. Remove the tumbler axis pin and tumbler, raise the sear, push the screwed head out of its way and the firing pin will drop out.

(5) *Gib, gib spring, or extractor spring.*—This will necessitate the removal of the extractor from the face of lock casing. Release the lock spring, drive out lock spring axis pin, remove keeper bracket, extractor levers, and lock spring, rotate tumbler to withdraw firing pin; next drive out keeper pin of extractor stop, remove latter and slide the extractor off the lock casing; push out gib spring cover, and remove the spring or gib, as the case may be. If extractor spring requires replacing drive out its fixing pin and remove.

Note.—The serviceable components are replaced in the reverse order.

Damaged parts of the lock, no spare part being available.

The gun will fire without the sear, or if the bents of the sear or firing pin are badly worn or broken off, but only single shots, and only by pressing and releasing the double button quickly.

The gun will also fire if the nose of the trigger or bent of the tumbler is badly worn or broken off, but only rapid firing. In this case the gun will fire the instant the crank handle reaches the check lever,- although the double button has not been pressed.

If necessary firing can be stopped by throwing the filled end of the belt over the breech casing to the left.

When firing has been stopped as described above, hold the crank handle with the right hand, open the cover, press down the horns of the extractor, draw the lock back and, if there is a live cartridge on the face of the extractor, remove the feed block and belt, close the cover, and allow the lock to fly forward, when the live cartridge, which is on the face of the extractor, will be fired. The lock can then be changed with safety. On no account should the lock be allowed to fly forward until the feed block has been removed and the cover shut.

If, on drawing the lock back, it is found that there is no live cartridge on its face, the lock may be changed at once and the necessity for removing the feed block and the subsequent precautions will not arise.

WEIGHTS OF SPRINGS, &C.

	lbs.	
Lock spring	12 to 14	Lock at full cock.
Gib spring	4 ,, 6	When upper nib is pressed down flush.
Extractor spring	4 ,, 6	When pressed down flush.
Fuzee spring	5 ,, 7	Lock cocked.
Fuzee spring (when muzzle attachment is fitted)	8 ,, 10	Lock cocked.
Ejector tube spring	2½ ,, 4	To push the case out of the tube. Gun stripped.
Recoiling portion	0 ,, 4	Gun level. Lock cocked and fuzee spring disconnected.
Converted Guns—		
Fuzee spring, Mk. I gun	10 ,, 12	Lock cocked.
Fuzee spring, Mk. II gun	5 ,, 7	Lock cocked.
Recoiling portion	0 ,, 7	Gun level. Lock cocked and fuzee spring disconnected.

Note.—The tension of the fuzee spring should always be kept as high as possible consistent with maintaining the normal rate of fire.

ADJUSTING CONNECTING ROD, Mk. II.

Five cotters; numbered 0, 1, 2, 3, 4; four washers; numbered 1, 2, 3, 4 are supplied. When necessary they can be fitted as follows, without stripping the gun:—

Turn the crank handle on to the buffer spring, raise the lock and allow it to rest on the rear cross-piece. Drive down the cotter, raise the lock to an upright position, pull out the cotter with the pliers, and take off the lock with the front part of the connecting rod attached. Now place the washer required over the stud on the boss; then rejoin the connecting rod. Insert the cotter of the same number as the washer used (from the top side), allow the lock to rest on the feed block, and drive the cotter to its place. When a combination of washers is used, the cotter belonging to the thickest washer of the combination should be employed.

Note.—The washers are of the following thicknesses:—No. 1 ·0025″, No. 2 ·005″, No. 3 ·01″, No. 4 ·02″.

EXAMINATION.

The following are the principal points to be observed in the examination of Maxim guns without using gauges:—

Recoiling portion.—See this moves freely. Pull not to exceed 4 lbs. (converted guns 7 lbs.).

Foresight.—See that the barleycorn is in good condition.

Tangent sight.—See that the top edge and V on leaf are in good condition, and that the slide works correctly.

Crank handle.—The crank should bear against the stops. To try this, remove lock and place a piece of thin paper between crank and stop. If the crank fails to nip the paper, the crank handle is probably bent, and bearing on the check lever or against the resistance piece.

Safety catch.—See the spring and catch act automatically when the firing lever is released.

Firing lever.—Test the firing lever by seeing that the trigger bar does not release the trigger before the safety catch is clear, and also see that the trigger is released before the stop on the lever bears against the stop on the rear cross piece.

Ejector tube.—See the spring grips a cartridge case.

Connecting rod, Mark II.—Test whether the correct washer is in, as follows:—Take off the fuzee spring. See that the spring cotter is in its place. Test the length of rod by raising the lock and putting one of the special dummy cartridges, issued to armourers, into the extractor over the firing pin hole; turn the crank handle on to the buffer spring, hold the extractor up against the top stop and let the crank handle come back slowly on to the check lever; if the rod is the correct length the crank handle will require a slight pressure of the hand to force it on to the check lever.

Steam tube.—See that the outer tube moves freely on inner tube when the gun is elevated and depressed.

Barrel.—See to the condition of rifling, lead and coppering.

Lock.—Test the extractor and side levers by bringing the crank handle gently on to the check lever. If the levers are correct, the extractor will be right up. Test the bents of the sear and firing pin. To do this, turn the crank handle on to the buffer spring, raise the safety catch, press the firing lever forward and keep it there. Then bring the crank handle gently down on to the check lever. The extractor should be well up to the top position before the firing pin is released. Examine the face of the extractor for burrs and flaws, at gaps, and firing pin hole. Try the grooves with a dummy cartridge (armourers' dummies must be used for this purpose) to see the gib holds the cartridge horizontally. See that the nose of the trigger and bent of the tumbler are not too much worn. See that the point and bent of the firing pin are in good condition. A broken firing pin can be recognized without stripping the lock by releasing the lock spring with the extractor up. If correct the firing pin will then protrude from the firing pin hole and can be withdrawn by depressing the tail of the tumbler. If broken it will remain protruding.

General.—See that all pins and fixing pins are correct.

ACTION OF THE MECHANISM.

The gun is prepared for rapid fire by hand, as follows :—

1st motion of crank handle.—On revolving the crank handle on to the buffer spring the lock is drawn to the rear, the extractor horns riding along the "solid cams" until they reach the ends of cams, when the extractor drops, partly by its own weight and assisted by the cover springs. The revolving of the crank adds to the *initial tension* of fuzee spring by the chain being wound round the fuzee, and on releasing the crank handle the fuzee spring causes the lock to fly forward, and the extractor, acted upon by the side and extractor levers, rises and seizes the cartridge which has been brought up into position by pulling the belt through the feed block from right to left with the left hand.

2nd motion of crank handle.—On again revolving the crank handle to the front the lock is drawn to the rear, taking with it the live cartridge from belt, the extractor drops, thus bringing the cartridge in line with the chamber, and on the lock going forward the second time this cartridge is placed in the chamber and the extractor rises to engage a second cartridge, which has been drawn into position in feed block as before detailed.

During the passage of lock to the rear the screwed head on side levers (due to the motion of crank) presses down the tail end of tumbler, revolving it on its axis pin, and causing its head, which is engaged with firing pin, to draw back the latter until its bent is engaged by the bent on sear, thus cocking the lock and compressing the lock spring between the firing pin and trigger. On going forward the screwed head and connecting rod tend to straighten themselves, and the former lifts the sear, leaving the firing pin held by the tumbler bent engaging with that of the trigger. The gun is now ready for *rapid fire.*

To fire.—On lifting the safety catch and pressing the firing lever the trigger bar is drawn to the rear; the bar engaging with the tail of trigger pulls it also to the rear, thus releasing the tumbler and firing pin; the latter acted upon by the lock spring flies forward, striking the cap of cartridge and firing the gun.

Immediately on firing, the pressure of gas causes the barrel and side plates to recoil for about 1 inch, and the arm on crank handle coming into contact with the resistance piece forces the curved face on crank handle to *roll* on the resistance piece and itself, thus imparting a rotary or downward motion to the crank ; this motion causes the lock to be drawn back and the crank handle to strike the buffer spring. At the same time as this motion is being imparted to the crank the fuzee winds the chain around it, thus further extending the fuzee spring. As the lock moves to the rear it takes the empty case from chamber and live cartridge from belt, the extractor drops, thus bringing empty case in line with ejector tube, and live cartridge in line with chamber where retained by extractor spring and gib. When the lock is right back, its flanges are clear of the guides on the side plates, and it is kept in position by the gunmetal block. The recoil of barrel and side plates imparts a lateral motion through the top and bottom levers to the feed block slide, and the pawls on slide engage a cartridge in the belt ready to bring it up into position in feed block. When the energy of recoil is absorbed the fuzee spring asserts itself and, assisted by the buffer spring rebound, carries side plates and barrel back into firing position, feeding up the cartridge, the spring unwinds the chain from fuzee revolving the crank and forcing the lock to its normal position, the extractor places empty case in ejector tube and live round in chamber, then rises and seizes another cartridge in feed block.

At the instant the extractor reaches the firing position the screwed head releases the sear and firing pin, the motions being continued so long as firing lever is kept pressed and trigger bar held back, until the ammunition in belt is expended.

Note.—To fire single shots only, revolve crank handle, pull belt through, and let go handle. This places live cartridge in extractor. Revolve crank a second time, *do not touch belt*, this places live cartridge in line with chamber, and on letting go crank handle the lock places it in chamber; extractor rises, but *does not engage another cartridge in feed block.* On firing, a fresh cartridge is fed up, and it will be only necessary to turn crank handle on to buffer spring to repeat the single shots.

Single shots can also be fired with the gun prepared for rapid fire by pressing the firing lever quickly, groups of four or five shots may also be fired, but this requires considerable practice.

STOPPAGES OR JAMS.

May be classed under two headings :—
I. *Temporary.*—Which are usually due to—
   (a) Failure of some part of the mechanism, which is generally duplicated, and therefore easily replaced, or it may be defective ammunition.
   (b) Want of knowledge of the working parts of the mechanism, or neglect in preparing for action.
II. *Prolonged.*—Due to breakages or defects in the mechanism, which require time and skilled assistance to put right, the gun being put out of action for a considerable period.

The cause of a stoppage or jam in the action of the gun during firing can, as a rule, be quickly detected by noting the position of crank handle, the position taken up by the latter showing teh exact place where the lock has been arrested in its backward or forward movement.

Whenever a stoppage occurs, first try to clear, if unsuccessful, see if barrel is home by ascertaining whether there is any space between the front edges of the crank bearings and breech casing, if the barrel is not home it will be due to either the "g.m. valve" working loose or a "fault in feed." The latter can be quickly ascertained, without opening cover, by feeling if the feed block slide is "fast" or "loose"—if the former a fault in feed is indicated, if the latter it is probably the valve that is at fault.

The above has reference to the more common "jams" that occur. There are, however, a number of incidental stoppages that the position of crank handle may or may not indicate; these are enumerated further on.

When a *Temporary* stoppage necessitates the replacement of a lock, feed block, or other spare component, the part removed should be repaired as soon as possible so as to make it again available for use.

If, when the cover is opened to investigate the cause of stoppage, it is seen that the extractor is not quite up, no attempt should be made to raise it. On the contrary, it should be first pushed down before the crank handle is turned over to the front, as by this means all risk of firing a cartridge accidentally is avoided.

Should it ever be necessary to release the lock spring with the lock out of the gun, this should be done with the extractor fully up, and the firing pin hole opposite the firing pin.

Temporary Stoppages.

I.	II.	III.	IV.	V.
Position of crank handle and its indication.	Immediate action.	Probable Cause.	Prevention of Recurrence.	Method of preparation for instructional purposes.
Indication. The lock is unable to come back far enough to allow the extractor to drop.	(i) Turn the crank handle on to the buffer spring, pull the belt to the left front, and let go the crank handle. (ii) If failure recurs, lighten fusee spring by 3 "turns."	The extractor has not dropped. This may be due to:— (*a*) Too heavy fusee spring. (*b*) Excessive friction, due to want of oil; grit or tight pockets in the belt, or excessive packing in cannelure or packing gland. (*c*) Partial loss of the force of the explosion due to:— (1) Worn barrel.	(*b*) Clean and oil working parts. Examine the belt, which should be dried if damp; of if the stoppage is due to a new or stiff belt, the pockets should be plugged. If due to excessive packing, examine and repack cannelure or packing gland.	Raise the lock, and place an empty case over the firing pin hole, and a dummy cartridge between the projections of the gib. Pull a cartridge into position in the feed block, replace lock with the horns of the extractor on the top of the solid cams. *For range purposes:—* Increase the weight of the fusee spring.

Note.—If the continued lightening of the fusee spring results in the crank handle stopping in the 3rd position, take muzzle attachment into use, and put fusee spring back to normal weight.

Temporary Stoppages—*continued*.

I. Position of crank handle and its indication.	II. Immediate action.	III. Probable Cause.	IV. Prevention of Recurrence.	V. Method of preparation for instructional purposes.
		(ii) Defective ammunition.	(c) (i) The barrel should be examined at the first opportunity and if much worn in the lead should be changed.	
II *Indication.* The lock is unable to go fully home after recoil.	(i) Force the crank handle on to the buffer spring. Open the cover and examine the cartridge on the face of the extractor. If a damaged cartridge, or an undamaged cartridge with the front portion of a separated case adhering to it, clear the face of the extractor and reload.	(i) (a) Damaged cartridge. The cartridge is unable to enter the chamber completely although it has commenced to do so. (b) Separated case with front portion adhering to undamaged cartridge.		(a) Damaged cartridge:— Place a bulged dummy cartridge between the projections of the gib. Place an empty case over the firing pin hole. Pull a dummy cartridge into position in the feed block. Replace the lock. *For range purposes:*— Place a bulged dummy cartridge in the belt.
	(ii) If an undamaged cartridge with no front portion of separated case adhering to it is found on the face of the extractor, clear the face of the extractor, and replace the lock, keeping the crank handle on the buffer spring. Take the clearing plug (seeing that the centre pin is back) and insert it into the chamber. Push the pin well home by allowing the lock to go forward. Then, keeping a firm pressure on the crank handle, give the clearing plug a rocking motion; withdraw the lock; lever back the handle of the clearing plug, withdraw it (seeing that the front portion of the separated case is on the clearing plug) and re-load.	(ii) Separated case. The front portion of the case causes an obstruction and prevents the next cartridge from going into the chamber.	(b) If a succession of separated cases occur the connecting rod must be lengthened.	(b) Separated case. Perform half the loading motions. Open the cover, withdraw and lift up the lock. Place the front portion of a separated case over the bullet of the cartridge on the extractor and the base portion of a separated case over the firing pinhole. Replace the lock, close the cover, pull the belt and let the crank handle go slowly back. *For range purposes:*— File a cartridge about 1 inch from the base and insert in the belt. Care must be taken that the cartridge is not filed too far through, as there is the danger of the bullet being left in the barrel.

Temporary Stoppages—continued.

I. Position of crank handle and its indication.	II. Immediate action.	III. Probable Cause.	IV. Prevention of Recurrence.	V. Method of preparation for instructional purposes.
III *Indication.* The extractor is unable to rise to its highest position. If the feed block slide is jammed, there is a fault in feed.	(i) Strike the crank handle on to check lever by a glancing bow with the palm of the hand. If failure recurs, strengthen the fusee spring by 3 turns. *Note.*—If the continued strengthening of the fusee spring results in the crank handle stopping in the first position, change the lock, putting the fusee spring back to normal; if failure recurs take muzzle attachment into use. (*See* para. 44.) (ii) If (i) fails, slightly raise the crank handle, pull the belt to the left front, let go the crank handle, and then strike it down on the check lever.	(i) (*a*) Too light fusee spring. (*b*) Excessive friction. (ii) A cartridge is fed up slightly crossways, or a long brass strip is bent.	(i) (*b*) Clean and oil working parts. (ii) Carefully examine the belt.	(1) Perform the correct loading motions, except that when completing the loading the crank handle must be eased back gently until it is in the 3rd position. (*See* diagram, Col. 1.) *For range purposes* :— Lighten the fusee spring. (ii) Perform half the loading motions, Place the crank handle on to the buffer spring. Open the cover, place an empty case over the firing pin hole, pull a cartridge half-way into position in the feed block, and holding it there, close the cover and let the crank handle go slowly back. *For range purposes* :— Bend a long brass strip.
	(iii) A. If (i) and (ii) fail, examine feed block slide. If jammed, No. 1 holds up the crank handle and opens the cover. No. 2, with the assistance of No. 1, removes the feed block, and replaces it by the spare one. Meanwhile No. 1 forces down the horns of the extractor, and places the crank handle on the buffer spring. As soon as the spare feed block is in position, No. 1 closes the cover and pulls the top cartridge of a fresh belt into position and lets go the crank handle.	(iii) A (1) Badly filled belt, or a belt with worn or loose pockets. The cartridges projecting unevenly from the belt prevent it entering or passing freely through the feed block. (iii) A. (2) Belt box not being in line with the feed block; the belt does not lead up correctly to the feed block and becomes jammed. *Note.*—The effect of a fault in feed is that the top pawls being engaged behind a cartridge in the belt are held fast when some obstruction, such as above, prevents the belt from passing freely through the feed block. The recoiling portions, being connected by the top and bottom levers to the slide, are arrested and prevented from going home. The distance they are held back depends upon the point at which the obstruction asserts itself.	(iii) A. (1) Carefully examine the new belt. (iii) A. (2) See that the new belt box is in line.	(iii) A. (1) Pull out the fourth cartridge in the belt about ¼ inch. Perform half the loading motions and hang the lock (*see* para. 51). Pull the crank handle to the rear and at the same time pull the belt to the left. Let go the crank handle, raise the lock and place a dummy cartridge between the projections of the gib, and an empty case over the firing pin hole. Replace the lock, shut the cover, and let go the crank handle. *For range purposes* :— Fill a belt badly. (iii) A. (2) *For range purposes* :— Place the belt box at an angle to the feed block.

Temporary Stoppages—*continued*.

I. Position of crank handle and its indication.	II. Immediate action.	III. Probable Cause.	IV. Prevention of Recurrence.	V. Method of preparation for instructional purposes.
Third—*continued*.	(iii) B. If free, No. 1 opens the cover. No. 2 forces down the horns of the extractor. No. 1 clears the face of the extractor, and changes the lock. He removes the cartridge in position in the feed block and re-loads.	(iii) B.(1) Damaged cartridge grooves. (2) Broken gib spring. (3) Broken gib. In these cases the extractor is prevented from rising to its highest position. It may be necessary sometimes to slide the cartridge or the empty case upwards, when clearing the face of the extractor. (4) Thick-rimmed cartridge. *Note*—If it is apparent that the stoppage is due to a thick-rimmed cartridge, it will not be necessary to change the lock.		(iii) B. Damage the rim of the leading dummy cartridge in the belt, pull it into position in the feed block. Place a dummy cartridge between the projections of the gib, and an empty case opposite the firing pin hole. Replace the lock. close the cover, and let go the crank handle. *For range purposes*:— Damage the rim of a *dummy* cartridge and place it in belt. *Note*.—(1) As damage to the extractor has to be simulated by damaging a cartridge rim, this cartridge must be removed before reloading. (2) This stoppage should seldom be practised *on the range*, since the thickened rim may cause damage to the grooves.
IV. *Indication*. That there has been no explosion, or, if any, that there has been little or no recoil, the lock remaining in its orward position.	(*a*) Turn the crank handle on to the buffer spring, pull the belt to the left front, and let go the crank handle. (*b*) If (*a*) fails, place the crank handle on to the buffer spring twice, change the lock, and reload.	(*a*) (1) No cartridge in the chamber. (2) Defective ammunition. (*b*) (1) Broken or damaged firing pin. (2) Broken lock spring.		(*a*) Load, and press the double button. *For range purposes*:— Place a dummy cartridge in the belt. (*b*) *For range purposes*:— The effect of these will be simulated by placing two dummy cartridges in the belt.

Note—Worn or damaged side or extractor levers may result in the extractor being unable to rise, or if the side levers are bent, there may either be a succession of separated cases, or the lock may become jammed.

Faults in Feed.

In nearly all cases the barrel will not be able to go right home, therefore the *crank bearings* will be *showing a space in front*, and *feed block slide* will be *stuck fast*.

Probable cause.—(1) Long cartridge (will not pass on to the cartridge and bullet stops). (2) Damaged cartridge (same as for last). (3) Badly filled belt. (4) Top pawls catching strips after last round has been fed up to ready position.

Jams also occur through the long strips getting bent, or cartridges jarring loose during firing, especially with an old or worn belt. If the belt box is at an undue angle a jam outside feed block will be the result.

Explanation.—The effect of a fault in feed is that the top pawls having engaged behind a cartridge in the belt are unable, owing to some obstruction, to carry the cartridge up to the bullet and cartridge stops in the feed block. The slide which carries these pawls is connected to the barrel, and the result is the latter is prevented from going home. The distance it is held back will depend on the position of the slide in block, so that the 3rd position of crank handle will not always be the position in which a fault in the feeding action occurs, but is most usual.

Remedy.—The quickest way to clear the above jams would be to remove the feed block and belt complete, and take the spare feed block and fresh belt into use.

The *jammed block and belt* meanwhile *being put right, ready for replacement* when a favourable opportunity occurs.

Miss-fires.

Miss-fires are usually caused through some of the following:—
(1) Worn point of firing pin. (2) Weak lock spring. (3) Side levers worn. (4) Extractor levers worn. (5) Bent on firing pin or sear worn (or shallow). (6) Defective or deteriorated ammunition.

In addition to the foregoing stoppages a varied number of other causes are given below in detail. They are not of a common occurrence, but have been known to happen, and are included here to enable a detachment to recognize them and apply such remedy as may be advisable.

Other Stoppages.

A { *At Rapid fire.*—1st Position of crank handle and *Barrel Home.* (1) Broken cover springs. (2) Broken firing pin at tumbler way, or recess for lock spring. (3) Broken head or tail of tumbler.

B { 3rd Position of crank handle with *Barrel Home.* (1) Heavy gib or extractor spring. (2) Strained firing pin or tumbler. (3) Slightly damaged cartridge. (4) Dirty or rusty chamber. (5) Tight packing. (6) Bad feed. (7) Side plates damaged or bent. (8) Buckled extractor spring. (9) Fouling or erosion in ball attachment. (10)

Firing pin hole in extractor burred. (11) Screwed head of lock not home. (12)* Gunmetal valve worked loose. (13) Mark II connecting rod too long.

C { 4th Position of crank handle, with *Barrel Home*. (1) Broken feed arm of side plate. (2) Broken stud on feed block slide. (3) Broken top or bottom lever of feed block. (4) Broken trigger bar at knuckle joint. (5) Shutter pivot screw worked loose or unscrewed.

D { AT SINGLE FIRE. 4th Position of crank handle. *Barrel not home.* (1) Heavy fuzee spring. (2) Light charge. (3) Want of oil. (4) Broken head or tail of tumbler. (5) Broken firing pin. (6) Barrel worn.

Stoppage may be caused by cotter working out.

With regard to the above stoppages, briefly explained:—
" A."—Denotes that the lock has recoiled, at least the full length of a cartridge, but the extractor has not dropped, or if it has, the bullet is not in line with the chamber. " B."—Denotes the inability of the extractor to rise after the lock has gone right forward. " C."—That the breech is properly closed; this can be readily distinguished from a " miss-fire " by the fact that it is possible to load by hand, and in case of 1, 2, and 3 to fire the gun without getting any " feed," and in the case of 4 and 5 not to hear the lock fire when the firing lever is pressed. " D."— The faults given are all liable to be brought about by loading the gun for *single fire*, but if the gun is set for *rapid fire* and *single shots* are fired deliberately by tapping the firing lever these faults would not occur; with 4 and 5 the " tumbler " and " firing pin " are damaged at the moment of firing. It should be noted that it is *single fire*, and the *barrel is not home.*

---

* The barrel will not go home.

⁕GUN, VICKERS', '303-in.

(Approved November 1912, L. of C., para. 16217.)

† Weight (with muzzle attachment)	...	$28\frac{1}{2}$ lbs.
Rate of Fire	...	500 rds. per min.
Sighted H.V. ammunition	... ...	2,900 yards.

Nomenclature of Parts of Gun.

‡ Barrel... ...	With asbestos packing.
§ Block, feed ...	Consisting of: Body; slide; top and bottom levers and split pin; top and bottom pawls (front and rear), springs and axis pins.
Box, fuzee spring	
* Casing, barrel...	Consisting of: Casing; steam tube with slide valve and keeper screw; packing gland; asbestos packing; two screwed plugs, each with link, S hook and stud; protector for condenser boss with chain and swivel; cork plug with chain and 2 S hooks; front protecting plate.
¶ *Casing, breech...	Consisting of: Casing; check lever, and keeper pin; sliding shutter with catch, keeper pin, spring and plunger; slide left; slide right, with roller, collar and split fixing pin; front cover catch, keeper pin, plunger, plug and spring.
Cover, front ...	
Cover, rear ...	Consisting of; Cover; cover lock, axis pin and spring; trigger bar and spring; cover joint pin with check nut and keeper pin.
Crank	With crank pin and fixing pin.
Fuzee	With chain and fixing pin.
Handle, crank...	With fixing pin.
Lock	Consisting of: Casing; side levers, axis bush and split pin; extractor levers, right and left; extractor; gib; gib spring and cover; sear and sear spring; trigger and axis pin; tumbler and axis pin; firing pin; lock spring (No. 1 or 2).
Plate, side, right	With side plate spring.
Plate, side, left	With side plate spring.

† Guns of later manufacture, in which a number of the lightening operations are omitted, weigh about $32\frac{1}{4}$ lbs. With barrel casing full of water the weight is increased by 10 lbs. The muzzle attachment weighs 1 lb.

‡ Mark I. or II. The latter is screwed at muzzle to take the Mark II. cup.

§ Steel or gunmetal.

¶ Earlier pattern (Mark I.) were fitted with piston and ring.

* These casings are riveted together.

Rear cross-piece...	Consisting of: Body; T fixing pin; joint pin, check nut and keeper pin; firing lever with pawl and axis pin; trigger bar lever; safety catch, axis pin, spring with piston; milled heads, with oil brushes and leather washers.
Rod, connecting...	With adjusting nut and 6 washers:—3, No. 1 (·003 in.); 3, No. 2 (·005 in.).
Sight, fore;	
Sight, tangent ...	Consisting of: Stem*; graduated plate (No. 1 for Mark VI., and No. 2 for Mark VII. ammunition) and upper and lower fixing screws; slide (Mark I. or II.); axis pin; tangent sight spring and piston. The Mark I. slide consists of: Slide; pinion, Mark I.; pawl and fixing pin; slide spring; milled head and fixing screw. The Mark II. slide consists of: slide; pinion, Mark II.; clamping nut and split pin; clamping screw and fixing pin.
Spring, fuzee ...	With fittings.
Screw, adjusting, fuzee spring	With vice pin.
Muzzle attachment, for ball firing.	Consisting of: Gland; cup, muzzle, Mark I. (with clamp screw) or II. (without screw, the cup being screwed to barrel); cone, front, Mark I. or II.; disc; outer casing with split keeper pin, chain, S-hook and stud; end cover, Mark I. or II., with chain and 2 S hooks.

Stripping the Gun.

The gun is stripped in the following order when on the mounting:—

Lock	Clear the extractor by revolving the crank handle twice; raise the rear cover, pull the crank handle on to the roller. See that the extractor drops, place finger between the extractor and stop, and thumb on rear end of the lock, lift lock—at the same time allowing the crank handle to move slowly forward until the lock is released from the side plates—give the lock $\frac{1}{6}$th turn, and lift out.

---

* Mark I. or II. The latter is provided at the joint end with an aperture sight, which is an integral part of the semi-circular flange, and is suitable for use with the existing pattern of foresight. It is sighted for a range of 400 yards, and is for use with stem in horizontal position. Guns fitted with Mark I. stems are provided with an independent fixed battlesight.

Block, feed	Release front cover catch, raise the cover, and lift out.
Box, fuzee, spring	With the right hand at the rear and the left hand at the front, press the box forward until clear of the lugs, and remove. Disconnect the fuzee chain and remove the box and the spring. Care should be taken to avoid throwing a cross strain on the chain.
Fuzee	Turn the fuzee to the rear until the lugs on the stem are free to be withdrawn.
Muzzle attachment.	Withdraw the split pin, give the outer casing $\frac{1}{6}$th turn and remove it. Next remove the end cover and unscrew the front cone. Loosen the clamping screw of the muzzle cup and revolve the cup till the clamping screw coincides with the flat on barrel. Remove the cup. Unscrew and remove the gland and packing.
Recoiling portion	Raise the rear cover, unscrew the rear crosspiece T fixing pin, and hinge down the cross-piece; remove slides right and left, and draw out the recoiling portion. Disconnect the side plates from the barrel (removing the left one first). If necessary, by taking out the fixing pin, the crank handle can be driven off with a drift and hammer; but, as a rule, this should not be stripped.
Roller	Remove split fixing pin, collar and roller.
Lever, check No. 1	Drive out keeper pin from underside, and take off check lever. To remove piston and spring, turn the piston until its lugs are free to pass along the slots, when the piston will be forced out by the pressure of the spring.
Lever, check No. 2	This has no piston or spring, but otherwise is stripped similarly to No 1.
Sight, tangent	Unscrew axis pin and ease out, remove tangent sight, piston and spring.
Lock, cover, rear	Unscrew axis pin and ease out, remove cover lock and spring.
Trigger bar	Remove spring and withdraw trigger bar.
Covers, front and rear	Remove keeper pin and check nut; force out joint pin and take off covers.
Catch, cover, front	To remove spring and plunger: Press the plug forward and give $\frac{1}{4}$ turn by means of a screwdriver, when the plug will be forced out by the spring, and before removing the plunger it must be turned so that the slots are free to pass the lugs in the catch. If necessary, by taking

	out the keeper pin the catch may be removed.
Rear cross-piece...	Remove keeper pin and check nut, force out joint pin and remove rear cross-piece.
Sight, fore ...	The position of the foresight should be carefully marked; drive the foresight out of the dovetail seating through the right-hand opening in the protector.

Take out the elevating and crosshead joint pin and disconnect the gun.

Steam tube ...	Up-end the gun so that it stands on the rear end of the breech casing.
	Remove the keeper screw and unscrew the steam tube.
Shutter, sliding ...	Press in the catch and force the shutter to the front until it is against the stop, then press in the plunger with a No. 3 punch and further force the shutter until it is clear of the breech casing.

Note.—The steam tube should not be removed if the valve is free.

Assembling the Gun.

Reverse all the foregoing operations with the exception that the recoiling portion must be replaced before the front packing and gland.

Care must be taken when re-assembling the steam tube that the acorn end is inserted into its seating. This is more easily assured by keeping the acorn end in contact with the adjacent channel formed by the corrugations of the barrel casing. The tube should screw home freely when in the correct position.

When replacing the Mark I. muzzle cup on the barrel the screw must coincide with the flat on the muzzle to allow the cup to pass. After the cup has been pushed home it must be given a half-turn to bring the clamping screw into the cannelure and away from the flat. It must then be screwed firmly up with the combination tool. Neglect of this will lead to the cup being broken or blown off.

When replacing the gland of the muzzle attachment care must be taken to see that it is screwed right home to the barrel casing; when not home the gland is liable to foul the muzzle cup when the barrel recoils, and thus cause damage to the cup. The split pin which fixes the outer casing of the attachment to the gland should be placed in the lowest hole.

Stripping Component Parts.
THE LOCK.

To cock the lock...	A convenient method of holding the lock to facilitate cocking, examining, &c., is as follows:—
	Rest the bottom of the lock on the fingers of the left hand, hold up the extractor with the forefinger and keep the thumb clear of the trigger.

To ease the lock spring	Place the second finger of the right hand round the neck of the side levers and the thumb on top of the lock clear of the trigger. Lifting on neck of side levers cocks the lock. With the left hand support the lock as detailed above. Press the neck of side levers down to release the sear. With the side of a screwdriver or similar implement force the trigger to the rear, meanwhile placing the thumb against the top rear end of lock.

Note.—See that the lock is cocked before replacing it in the gun.

Side levers ...	Force out the split keeper pin and axis bush, turn side levers to clear extractor levers and remove.
Extractor levers, left and right	Lift off pivot.
Extractor... ...	Slide off.

Release the lock spring.

Tumbler and trigger	Press out the axis pins and remove.
Lock spring ...	Remove.
Firing pin ...	Raise sear and allow firing pin to slide out.
Sear with spring...	Remove.
Gib and spring ...	Push out the gib spring cover and remove.

Assembling.
In reverse order.

Note.—It will be found more convenient to replace the lock spring last, with the lock in the fired position.

THE FEED BLOCK.

Bottom lever ...	Drive out the split pin and tap out.
Top lever ...	Remove.
Slide with pawls and spring	Take out and remove pawls and spring.
Bottom pawls and spring	Draw out axis pin and remove.

Assembling.
In reverse order.

THE REAR CROSSPIECE.

Firing lever with pawl	Unscrew axis pin and remove.
Safety catch with spring and piston	Unscrew axis pin and remove
Trigger bar lever	Lift out.

Assembling.

In reverse order.

Note.—That the pawl engages trigger bar lever.

THE TANGENT SIGHT.

Milled head for Mark I. slide	Remove fixing screw and lift off.
Slide Mark I. & II.	Remove top fixing screw of graduated plate and run slide off the stem.
Slide spring for Mark I. slide	Remove.
Pawl and pinion for Mark I. slide	Press out fixing pin and remove from slide.
Graduated plate...	Unscrew bottom fixing screw and remove.
Clamping nut for Mark II. slide	Remove split pin and unscrew.

Assembling.

In reverse order.

WEIGHTS OF SPRINGS, &C.

	lbs.	
Lock spring	12 to 14	Lock at full cock.
Gib spring	4 ,, 6	When pressed down flush.
Fuzee spring	5 ,, 7	Lock removed and check lever held clear of the crank handle.
Fuzee spring (when ball attachment is fitted)	7 ,, 9	Lock removed and check lever held clear of the crank handle.
Recoiling portion	0 ,, 4	Gun level. Lock cocked and fuzee spring disconnected.

Testing and Adjusting Connecting Rod.

Take off fuzee spring. Raise cover and turn crank handle back.

The extractor being down, insert through opening in the underside of casing the special armourer's M.G. dummy cartridge in bottom end of extractor over firing pin hole.

Raise extractor, see that the barrel is home, turn crank handle on to the check lever, meanwhile guiding cartridge into chamber.

Push check lever back just clear of crank handle and let crank handle gently down towards rest.

If connecting rod is correct for length a slight check will be felt.

If no pressure is required, it shows that the lock is not fully home (*i.e.* that the connecting rod is not long enough) and in this event the connecting rod must be lengthened by the addition of washers Nos. 1 or 2 (or both) as may be required.

No. 1 washer ('003") has one small hole punched in rim.
No. 2 washer ('005") has two small holes punched in rim.

ACTION OF THE MECHANISM.

Note.—Before loading or firing the Vickers Gun, always see that the sliding shutter is fully back.

The gun is prepared for rapid fire as follows:—

First Motion of Crank Handle.—On revolving the crank handle on to the roller, the lock is drawn to the rear, the extractor horns riding along the solid cams until they reach the ends of cams, when the extractor drops, partly by its own weight and partly assisted by the ramps. The revolving of the crank adds to the initial tension of fusee spring by the chain being wound round the fusee, and on releasing the crank handle the fuzee spring causes the lock to fly forward, and the extractor, acted upon by the side and extractor levers, rises and seizes the cartridge, which has been brought into position by pulling the belt through the feed block from right to left with the left hand.

Cocking of Lock.—During the passage of the lock to the rear, the head of side levers—due to the motion of the crank—presses up the tail end of the tumbler, revolving it on its axis pin and causing its head, which is engaging with firing pin, to draw back the latter until its bent is engaged by the bent on sear, thus cocking the lock and compressing the lock spring between the firing pin and trigger. On going forward the head of side levers and connecting rod tend to straighten themselves, and the former releases the sear, leaving the firing pin held by the tumbler bent engaging with the nose of the trigger.

Second Motion of Crank Handle.—On again revolving the crank handle to the rear the lock is drawn back, taking with it the live round from belt, the extractor drops, thus bringing the cartridge in line with the chamber, and on the lock going forward the second time the cartridge is placed in the chamber and the extractor rises to engage a second cartridge which has been drawn into position in feed block as before detailed. The gun is now ready for rapid fire.

Action on Firing.—On lifting the safety catch and pressing the firing lever, the trigger bar lever is operated and the trigger bar is drawn to the rear; the bar engaging with the tail of trigger pulls it also to the rear, thus releasing the tumbler and firing pin; the latter, acted upon by the lock spring, flies forward, striking the cap of the cartridge and firing the gun. Immediately on firing the explosion will cause the recoiling portion to move backwards through a distance of one inch, thereby extending the fusee spring. This backward movement is due partly to recoil and partly to the effect of the ball-firing attachment, which acts as follows:—The powder gases which escape from the muzzle after the exit of the bullet strike violently against the front cone and rebound on to the front face of the muzzle cup, driving it and the barrel, to which it is attached, backward. The gases then escape into the air through the openings in the outer casing. As the recoiling portions move to the rear, the tail of the crank handle coming into contact with the roller, forces the curved tail of crank handle to roll on the roller, thus imparting a rotary or upward motion to the crank; this motion causes the lock to be drawn back and the crank handle itself to come into contact with the roller.

At the same time that this motion is being imparted to the crank the fusee winds the chain around itself, thus further extending the fusee spring. As the lock moves to the rear it takes the empty case from the chamber and a live cartridge from the belt, the extractor dropping and thus bringing the live cartridge in line with the chamber where it is retained by the gib, the spent case dropping from the extractor through aperture in breech casing to the ground by its own weight, or being forced off by fouling the seating at rear end of barrel casing as extractor rises. The lock is kept in position by means of flanges working along guides on the side plates and by the guides on the underside of the rear cover.

The recoil of barrel and side plates imparts a lateral motion through the top and bottom levers to the feed block side, and the pawls on slide engage a cartridge in the belt ready to bring it up into position in feed block. While the lock is still travelling to the rear, the continued rolling of crank handle against the roller causes the recoiling parts to move forward with the assistance of the fusee spring, causing the cartridge to be fed into position in the feed block; the spring unwinds the chain from the fusee, revolving the crank and forcing the lock into its normal position; the extractor places the live cartridge into the chamber and then rises and seizes another cartridge in the feed block. At the instant the extractor reaches the firing position the head of side levers releases the sear and firing pin, and the gun again fires. The foregoing motions are continued so long as the firing lever is kept pressed and trigger bar held back, until the ammunition in belt is expended.

To Fire Single Shots Only.—Revolve crank handle, pull belt through, and let go crank handle. This places a live cartridge in the extractor. Then revolve crank handle a second time, but without touching the belt. This places cartridge in line with chamber, and on letting go the crank handle the lock places the cartridge into chamber; the extractor rises, but does not engage another cartridge in feed block. On firing, a fresh cartridge is fed up, and it will be necessary only to turn crank handle on to roller and repeat the single shots. Single shots can also be fired with the gun prepared for rapid fire by pressing the firing lever quickly, and groups of four or five may also be fired, but this requires considerable practice.

Temporary Stoppages, Gun, Vickers, ·303-inch.

I.	II.	III.	IV.	V.
Position of crank handle and its indication.	Immediate action.	Probable Cause.	Prevention of Recurrence.	Method of preparation for instructional purposes.
I *Indication.*— The lock is unable to come back far enough to allow the extractor to drop.	(i) Turn the crank handle on to the roller, pull the belt to the left front, and let go the crank handle. (ii) If failure recurs lighten fusee spring by 3 " clicks."	The extractor has not dropped. This may be due to :— (a) Too heavy fusee spring. (b) Excessive friction, due to want of oil; grit, or tight pockets in the belt, or excessive packing in the cannelure or packing gland. (c) Partial loss of the force of the explosion due to :— (i) Worn barrel. (ii) Defective ammunition.	(b) Clean and oil working parts. Examine the belt, which should be dried if damp ; or if the stoppage is due to a new or stiff belt, the pockets should be plugged. If due to excessive packing, examine, and repack cannelure or packing gland. (c) (i) The barrel should be examined at the first opportunity, and, if much worn in the lead, should be changed.	Perform half the loading motions ; pull the crank handle slowly back until the horns of the extractor have engaged with the steps on the solid cans ; pull the belt to the left front, and let go the crank handle. *For Range Purposes.*—Increase the weight of the fusee spring.
II *Indication.*— The lock is unable to go fully home after recoil.	(i) Force the crank handle to the rear ; open the rear cover and examine the cartridge on the face of the extractor. If a damaged cartridge, or an undamaged cartridge with the front portion of a separated case adhering to it, clear the face of the extractor and reload. (ii) If an undamaged cartridge, with no front portion of separated case adhering to it is found on the face of the extractor, clear the face of the extractor, replace the lock keeping the crank handle on the roller. Take the clearing plug (seeing that the centre pin is back) and insert it into the chamber. Push the pin well home by allowing the lock to go forward. Then, keeping a firm pres-	(i) (a) Damaged cartridge. The cartridge is unable to enter the chamber completely although it has commenced to do so. (b) Separated case with front portion adhering to undamaged cartridge. (ii) Separated case. The front portion of the case causes an obstruction and prevents the next cartridge from going into the chamber.	(b) If a succession of separated cases occur the connecting rod must be lengthened (see para. 80).	(a) Bulge the leading dummy cartridge in the belt and load. *For Range Purposes.*— Place a bulged dummy cartridge in the belt. (b) Perform half the loading motions. Open the rear cover, withdraw and lift up the lock. Place the front portion of a separated case over the bullet of the cartridge on the extractor. Replace the lock, close the rear cover, pull the belt, and let the crank handle go slowly forward. *For Range Purposes.* — File a cartridge about one inch from the base, and insert in the belt. Care must be taken that the cartridge is not filed too far through, as

Temporary Stoppages, Gun, Vickers, ·303-inch—*continued*.

II—*continued*.

I. Position of crank handle and its indication.	II. Immediate action.	III. Probable Cause.	IV. Prevention of Recurrence.	V. Method of Preparation for Instructional Purposes.
	sure on the crank handle, give the clearing plug a rocking motion; withdraw the lock; lever back the handle of the clearing plug and withdraw it (seeing that the front portion of the separated case is on the clearing plug) and reload.			there is the danger of the bullet being left in the barrel.
III. *Indication.*— The extractor is unable to rise to its highest position. If the feed block slide is jammed, there is a fault in feed.	(i) Strike the crank handle on to the check lever by a glancing blow with the palm of the hand.	(i) Excessive friction.	(1) Clean and oil working parts.	(i) Perform the correct loading motions, except that when completing the loading the crank handle must be eased forward gently until it is in the 3rd Position (*see* diagram, col. 1). *For Range Purposes.*—Lighten the fusee spring.
	(ii) If (i) fails, slightly raise the crank handle, pull the belt to the left front, let go the crank handle, and then strike it down on the check lever.	(ii) A cartridge is fed up slightly crosswise or a long brass strip is bent.	(ii) Carefully examine the belt.	(ii) Perform half the loading motions. Pull the crank handle on to the roller. Open the rear cover, pull a cartridge half way into position in the feed block and hold it there, and let the crank handle go slowly forward. Close the cover. *For Range Purposes.*—Bend a long brass strip.
	(iii) A. If (i) and (ii) fail, examine feed block slide ; *if jammed* No. 1 pulls the crank handle on to the roller, (*), holds it there and unlocks the front cover. No. 2 opens the front cover, and with the assistance of No. 1 raises the feed block sufficiently to allow the recoiling portions to go home. He releases the top and bottom pawls from the belt, which he withdraws until the top cartridge is clear of the feed block and rectifies the belt	(iii) A. (i). Badly-filled belt with worn or loose pockets. The cartridges. projecting unevenly from the belt prevent it entering or passing freely through the feed block.	(iii). A. (i). Carefully examine belt.	(iii). A. (i). Pull out the fourth cartridge in the belt about ¼-inch. Perform half the loading motions; pull the crank handle slowly back until the horns of the extractor have engaged with the steps on the solid cams. Draw the recoiling portions to the rear by forcing the knob of the crank handle forward, and tail to the rear, at the same time pulling the belt to the left. Allow the recoiling,

Temporary Stoppages, Gun, Vickers, ·303-inch—*continued*

III—*continued.*

I.	II.	III.	IV.	V.
Position of crank handle and its indication.	Immediate action.	Probable Cause.	Prevention of Recurrence.	Method of preparation for Instructional purposes.
	or cartridges if necessary. He replaces the feed block, pushing the slide over to the left, and lowers the front cover. No. 1 locks the front cover, pulls the belt to the left front, and releases the crank handle. (*) *N.B.*—In order to do this, it may sometimes be necessary for No. 2 to open the front cover and force down the horns of the extractor.			portions to go forward. Bring the crank handle on to the roller and let go. *For Range Purposes.*—Fill a belt badly.
		(iii) A. (ii). Belt box not being in line with the feed block, the belt does not lead up correctly to the feed block and becomes jammed. *Note*—The effect of a fault in feed is that the top pawls, being engaged behind a cartridge in the belt, are held fast, when some obstruction, such as above, prevents the belt from passing freely through the feed block. The recoiling portions, being connected by the top and bottom levers to the slide, are arrested and prevented from going home. The distance they are held back depends upon the point at which the obstruction asserts itself.	(iii) A. (ii). See that the belt box is in line.	(iii). A. (ii). *For Range Purposes.*—Place the belt box at an angle to the feed block.
	(i). B. If *free*, No. 2 opens the front cover and forces down the horns of the extractor. No. 1 clears the face of the extractor, and changes the lock. He removes the cartridge in position in the feed block and reloads.	(iii). B. (1) Damaged cartridge grooves. (2) Broken gib spring (3) Broken gib. In these cases, the extractor is prevented from rising to its highest position. It may be necessary sometimes to slide the cartridge upwards when clearing the face of the extractor (4) Thick-rimmed cartridge. *Note.*—If it is apparent that the stoppage is due to a thick-rimmed cartridge, it will not be necessary to change the lock.		(iii). B. Damage the rim of the second dummy cartridge in the belt. Proceed to load. *For Range Purposes.*—Damage the rim of a *dummy* cartridge, and place it in the belt. *Notes.* — (1) As damage to the extractor has to be simulated by damaging a cartridge rim, this cartridge must be removed before reloading. (2) This stoppage should seldom be practised *on the range*, since the thickened rim may cause damage to the grooves.

Temporary Stoppages, Gun, Vickers, ·303-inch—*continued.*

Position of crank handle and its indication.	II. Immediate action.	III. Probable Cause.	IV. Prevention of Recurrence.	V. Method of preparation for instructional purposes.
IV. *Indication.*—That there has been no explosion, or, if any, that there has been little or no recoil, the lock remaining in its forward position.	(*a*) Turn the crank handle on to the roller, pull the belt to the left front and let go the crank handle. (*b*) If (*a*) fails, place crank handle on to the roller twice, change the lock and reload.	(*a*) (1) No cartridge in the chamber. (2) Defective ammunition. (*b*) (1) Broken or damaged firing pin. (2) Broken lock spring.		(*a*) Load and press the thumb pieces. *For Range Purposes.* — Place a dummy cartridge in the belt. (*b*) *For Range Purposes.*—The effect of these will be simulated by placing two dummy cartridges in the belt.

Note.—Worn, or damaged side or extractor levers may result in the extractor being unable to rise, or, if the side levers are bent, there may be either a succession of separated cases, or the lock may become jammed.

GUN, LEWIS, ·303-IN.
(Approved October, 1915. L. of C., Para. 17484.)
GENERAL DESCRIPTION.

Weights:—
Gun ... ... 26 lb.
Magazine, filled (except Mark II)   4 lb. 5 oz.
„   empty... ... ...   1 lb. 11 oz.

Dimensions:—
Length (with stock butt) ... 4 feet $2\frac{5}{8}$ inches.
„ (without stock butt) ... 3 „ $4\frac{5}{8}$ „
Extreme width ... ... $4\frac{1}{2}$ inches.

Sighting.—The gun is sighted up to 2,000 yards for Mark VII ammunition. When firing Mark VI ammunition an addition to the actual range, to the extent of 250 yards for ranges up to 1,000 yards and 300 yards for ranges over 1,000 yards, must be placed on the sight.

The gun can be fired from the service mountings when the latter are fitted with an adapter.

Magazines.—The gun is fed by flat circular magazines, of which Nos. 1, 2, 5 and 6, Mark I are for use in the field, and Nos. 3, 4 and 7, Mark I, for air service. These hold 47 rounds each.

A Mark II magazine, converted from either No. 1, 2 or 3 Mark I, and holding 97 rounds, has recently been introduced for Air Service.

The No. 3 Mark I magazine has a finger piece hinged to the magazine catch, and the other air service magazines have a leather handle and catch attached to brackets riveted to the centre disc to enable the magazine to be manipulated with one hand.

Components.—The gun may be considered to be divided into two portions, stationary and moving, and is worked automatically by two forces: (1) the pressure of the gas resulting from the explosion of the charge, and (2) the return spring. The main components of the gun are:—

Stationary.—Body, barrel, radiator, radiator casings, body cover and tangent sight, gas cylinder, gas chamber, gas regulator, trigger guard and butt, or spade handle grip.

Moving.—Piston rod, bolt with actuating stud, return spring and feed arm.

The barrel is encircled by an aluminium radiator, having longitudinal flanges. This radiator is covered by front and rear casings, the front casing projecting about 5 inches beyond the muzzle of the barrel. Through these casings the cold air is sucked by the rush of gas from the muzzle. Radiation from the flanges, assisted by this rush of cold air, tends to keep the gun cool.

Mechanism.—The gun is gas operated. When the gun is fired, gases escape through a vent hole in the forward portion of barrel, and, impinging on the head of the piston, force the piston rod and bolt to the rear until the nose of the sear engages in bent on the rear portion of piston. This operation causes the return spring to be compressed by the rack on the piston acting on the pinion containing the return spring. To allow the recoiling portions to move forward the trigger is pressed. This releases the nose of the sear from the piston, and the return spring coming into play, forces the piston and bolt forward: the bolt pushes a cartridge into the chamber. A further movement of the piston carries the point of the striker on to the cap of the cartridge. During the motion of the bolt a projection on the feed arm actuating stud moves the feed arm, thus causing the rotation of the magazine.

Nomenclature of Parts.

The following is the nomenclature of parts of the gun:—

Barrel	With barrel mouthpiece and band for attachment of gas chamber.
Body	With ejector and ejector cover; body lock pin; pinion casing hinge pin; and safety catch plates, left and right.
Body cover ...	With cartridge guide; and stop pawls, right and left, and spring.
Bolt	With two extractors.
Butt	With butt cap and screw; and butt plate and two screws.
Clamp Ring ...	With screw and foresight.
Feed arm ...	With pawl and spring; and latch.
Feed arm actuating stud.	
Gas chamber.	
Gas cylinder.	
Gas regulator ...	With key.
Pinion casing ...	With pinion; return spring and casing; hub; tension screw; and pinion pawl, axis pin, and spring.
Piston rod ...	With rack and fixing pin; striker and fixing pin; and cocking handle.
Radiator.	
Radiator casing	Front and rear.
Tangent sight...	With axis pin and washer; leaf; spring; slide; and elevating screw with milled head, keeper pin, and check spring.
Trigger guard and pistol grip.	With trigger; trigger axis pin; trigger spring; plunger; sear; sear axis pin; butt catch and spring; and butt catch fixing pin.

The following is the nomenclature of parts of the magazine:—

Magazine ...	With pan; separating pegs; centre disc; centre block; and catch with spring.

STRIPPING AND ASSEMBLING.

To strip the gun.—The gun is stripped in the following order:—

Notes.—(1) Operations marked with an asterisk being required only for the replacement of worn or broken parts must not be undertaken for instructional purposes more frequently than is necessary to make the method of such replacement understood.

(2) A live or dummy cartridge with pointed bullet will be found the most useful tool for stripping.

Butt.—Insert the point of a bullet behind the catch and press it upwards to disengage the catch. Then rotate the butt one-eighth of a turn in a direction contrary to that of the hands of a clock and withdraw the butt.

Trigger guard and pistol grip.—Press the trigger to disengage the sear nose and plunger from their holes in the bottom of the body and slide the guard back till it is clear of the body.

Bolt and piston rod.—Draw back the cocking handle to its full extent and withdraw it from the piston rod by pulling it outwards. Draw out the bolt and piston rod.

Body cover.—See that the feed arm is over to the right, draw back the body cover till it is clear of its retaining surfaces on the body and lift it off.

Feed arm.—With the point of a bullet press forward the latch. Turn the feed arm till the key way in the axis hole clears the key on the magazine post and lift it off.

Body.—With the point of a bullet press back the body locking pin. To do this the pinion casing must be allowed to drop, but not quite to its full extent, to permit the pin to move back. Unscrew the body from the barrel.

After the rear face of the barrel is removed from the protection afforded by the body, great care must be taken to preserve the projections on it from damage. The barrel and radiator should never be stood muzzle upwards on any hard surface.

Pinion casing.—Remove the body locking pin and unhook the pinion casing.

Gas regulator.—With the point of a bullet lift the key till the stud on its end is clear of the hole in the radiator casing. Remove the key and unscrew the gas regulator.

Gas chamber plug for Mark II. gas chambers.—Using a screwdriver, unscrew the keeper screw, and with the spanner unscrew the plug. *This has a left-handed thread, and must be turned as when screwing up an ordinary screw.*

Clamp ring and front radiator casing.—Unscrew the fixing screw and remove the clamp ring and front radiator casing.

Rear radiator casing.—Slide the casing off to the rear.

Gas cylinder.—Insert the piston rod till the rack enters the cylinder and, using it as a wrench, unscrew the gas cylinder.

*Gas chamber.—Using the spanner, unscrew the gas chamber Mark I.

Gas chamber Mark II.—The gas chamber plug having been unscrewed as above, the gas chamber will drop out when the barrel is withdrawn from the radiator.

Barrel mouthpiece.—Using the spanner unscrew the barrel mouthpiece. *This has a left-handed thread and must be turned as when screwing up an ordinary screw.*

Radiator.—Assemble the jack collar and the screw jack to the barrel by means of the breech thread, and with a hammer give the projecting arm of the jack a sharp blow to tighten the jack against the collar. This will start the barrel out from the radiator, which can then be withdrawn.

Band.—When the barrel comes away the band is left in the radiator and can be removed.

Assembling the gun.—Reverse the above operation. In replacing the barrel and radiator in the rear casing great care must be taken to avoid damaging the projections on the rear face of the barrel. Similar care must be exercised in replacing screwed portions, particularly the gas chamber, cylinder, and barrel mouthpiece.

Before replacing the body cover it must be seen that the feed arm is over to the right.

When raising the pinion casing into position it may be necessary to move the cocking handle slightly to make the pinion and rack engage together properly. Want of engagement between these parts will make it impossible to slide the trigger guard into position.

STRIPPING VARIOUS COMPONENTS.

The various components are stripped as follows:—

* *Trigger guard.*—To remove the sear, press out its axis pin. To remove the trigger, plunger, or spring, press out the trigger axis pin. To remove the butt catch, press out the fixing pin.

* *Bolt.*—To remove an extractor, lift the hook till the stud is disengaged from its recess, and push the extractor out of the slot in the bolt. Care must be taken not to strain the extractor or its seating by raising the hook higher than is necessary.

* *Body cover.*—With the point of a bullet force the stud on the pawl spring out of its seating in the transverse rib, Lift the pawls off their studs.

Note.—Studs and pawls are marked " 1 " and " 2 " to ensure that the pawls are assembled in the proper position.

Press the stud of the cartridge guide down, and slide the spring out of its seating. Unscrew the fixing screw and remove the tangent sight bed and tangent sight.

* *Feed arm.*—Lift the pawl off its stud and remove the spring.

* *Body.*—With the point of a bullet raise the rear end of the ejector cover and slide it to the rear. Remove the ejector.

Pinion and return spring.—Press up the horizontal arm of the pinion pawl to release the spring. Unscrew the tension screw and remove the pinion from its casing. With the point of a bullet press on the hub and push the return spring casing out of the pinion. Press out the pinion pawl axis pin and remove the pawl and spring.

Note.—In order to replace a broken pinion or return spring it is not necessary to remove the body cover or feed arm. After pushing back the body locking pin the body need only be rotated sufficiently to allow the locking pin to be pushed fully forward, when the pinion casing can be unhooked from its hinge pin.

Foresight.—Using a punch drive the foresight out of its dovetail groove in the foresight block from left to right.

Tangent sight.—When the sight bed is removed from the body cover the spring can be tapped forward and removed. No other part of the sight must be removed except by an armourer.

ACTION OF MECHANISM.

After placing magazine in position on magazine post the gun is cocked by drawing back the cocking handle, thus drawing back the piston rod. During the first $1\frac{1}{2}$ inches of travel the bolt and feed arm remain stationary, but the rack causes the pinion to rotate, partly compressing the return spring. From this point for a further $1\frac{1}{3}$ inches the right side of the striker post, working against the cam face of the slot in the bolt, rotates the bolt so that the lugs are clear of their recesses in the body. The rear of the striker post then comes against the rear end of the slot in the bolt and the further backward travel carries back the bolt. Also, the boss on the feed arm actuating stud, working in the groove in the under side of the feed arm, carries the latter over to the left. The feed arm pawl, which is engaged behind one of the projecting portions on the rim of the magazine, carries the magazine pan round with it and a cartridge is thereby forced down the slope in the magazine centre block till its bullet end is free, when it drops on to the cartridge opening in the feed arm. The tongue on the body cover ensures that the cartridge is made to fall clear of the centre block of the magazine if it does not drop by its own weight. From this point the cartridge is carried to the left by the separating pegs and the indentations of the magazine, aided by the right side of the cartridge opening in the feed arm, till it reaches the cartridge opening in the body, by which time it has been forced under the cartridge guide (spring) and is clear of the pegs and indentations of the magazine. The stop on the left side of the feed arm ensures that the cartridge lies properly over the opening in the feed arm and is not carried beyond it. During this motion the spring stud on the feed arm passes away from the right stop pawl, which is then pressed forward by its spring and prevents the magazine from rotating too far. When the lug on the left of the feed arm actuating stud reaches the tail of the ejector it forces it inwards, thus forcing the head outwards. As the end of the travel of the piston rod is neared the bent in rear of the rack rides over the nose of the sear, depressing it. When the bent has passed, the nose of the sear rises again under the influence of the trigger spring. The rod and bolt then come against the butt cap and can travel no further back. The feed arm has then been carried fully over to the left and the cartridge has been brought over the cartridge opening in the top of the body, into which it is forced by the pressure of the cartridge guide (spring). The left stop pawl, which has been pressed rearwards by the rotation of the magazine, springs forward again and prevents any rotation of the magazine in a contrary direction. During the whole of the backward movement of the piston rod the rack has caused the rotation of the pinion and the consequent compression of the return spring.

The return spring now comes into play and drives the piston rod forward till the nose of the sear engages with the bent and stops the movement.

Effect of the Return Spring and of the Ignition of the Charge.— When the trigger is pressed the nose of the sear is lowered and released from contact with the bent on the piston rod. The return spring then comes into play and rotates the pinion, thus forcing the rod forward. The striker post now being lodged in the recess at the rear of the slot in the bolt, and the bolt not being able to turn by reason of the guide grooves in which the lugs work, the bolt is carried forward with the piston rod. The feed arm actuating stud is carried forward with the bolt, forcing the feed arm to the right. During this movement the feed arm pawl passes over the projection on the rim of the magazine and engages behind it, while the spring stud on the feed arm presses the right stop pawl back out of the path of the magazine. As the bolt-head passes the head of the ejector it forces it inwards, thus causing the tail to project into the bolt way. When the face of the bolt meets the base of the cartridge which is lying in the cartridge opening it pushes it before it into the chamber and the extractors spring over its rim. As soon as the bolt lugs are clear of the guides the striker post leaves the recess in the rear end of the slot in the bolt and its left side works against the cammed portion of the left side of the slot, rotating the bolt and causing the lugs to enter their recesses in the body, thus locking the bolt. The piston rod still continues to fly forward, and carries the point of the striker on to the cap, igniting the cartridge.

As a result of the ignition of the cartridge the bullet passes up the bore. When its base is clear of the gas hole in the barrel, a portion of the gas rushes with great force through the hole into the gas chamber and thence through the hole in the gas regulator on to the head of the piston rod, driving the rod back with great force. As a result the whole of the operations described above under the head of loading take place automatically, without the cocking handle being pulled, with the addition that as the bolt moves back the extractors withdraw the empty case from the chamber and carry it back on the face of the bolt. When the proper point is reached the tail of the ejector is forced inwards and the head is thus brought into collision with the case, which it throws out to the right through the ejection opening in the body.

If after the trigger is pressed it is released very rapidly, the sear nose has time to rise and it accordingly intercepts the bent in rear of the rack and holds the piston rod and bolt in their backward position. Single shots are fired in this manner, but the action of the gun is so rapid that the trigger must be instantaneously released after the pressure, or two or more shots will be fired.

If pressure is maintained on the trigger the sear nose is kept depressed, and there is no obstacle to the piston rod and bolt flying forward, so that the backward and forward movement is not interrupted until the trigger is released or the magazine is empty.

STOPPAGES.

Stoppages in the automatic action of the gun during firing may be classed under two main headings :—

(i.) *Temporary*, which are due to :—
- (a) Defective ammunition.
- (b) Failure of some part of the mechanism of which a duplicate is carried and which can therefore be easily and quickly replaced.
- (c) A fault in feed.
- (d) Some cause which can generally be avoided by a high standard of training and by a thorough knowledge of the gun on the part of the detachment. These are generally due to neglect of some of the points to be observed before, during, and after firing.

(ii.) *Prolonged*, which are due to failure of some part of the gun which cannot, as a rule, be put right by the detachment under fire or without skilled assistance. These necessarily put the gun out of action for a more or less prolonged period.

On the knowledge and training of the detachment depends the rapidity with which temporary stoppages can be overcome. A thorough understanding of their cause will give the detachment a practical knowledge of the working of the mechanism. Stoppages which produce the same effect as regards the position of the cocking handle may arise from various causes, and the reason of the stoppage must therefore be carefully studied and explained.

The following table of temporary stoppages, set out in five columns, gives an indication of the method of recognising the cause of the stoppage, based on the position of the cocking handle when the gun stops firing. The column headed "Immediate action" shows what should be done by the firer to clear the stoppage, while that headed "Prevention of recurrence" indicates what is necessary if the "Immediate action" does not prove successful. A further column gives the method of reproducing the stoppage for instructional purposes, whether with dummy cartridges, or on the range when firing ball ammunition, where reproduction is possible or desirable. This column is for the information of the instructor and its details need not be known by the detachment.

Whenever instruction is being carried out dummy cartridges in a magazine will always be used, and, in order to stimulate the various stoppages, empty cartridge cases, bulged and damaged dummy cartridges and portions of separated cases will be required by the instructors.

The instructor must see that the spare parts and tools are at hand when instruction is being carried out, whether in barracks or on the range, to enable stoppages to be remedied.

As the remedying of a stoppage often throws the sights off the target, the instructor should insist on the importance of relaying the gun, and for this purpose the instructional machine gun or landscape target must be used.

When the remedying of a stoppage involves the use of a spare part, the defective part which has been removed from the gun should, when possible, be repaired at the earliest opportunity to make it again serviceable.

In the table which follows it is taken for granted that the trigger will always be released before any attempt is made to remedy a stoppage. When it is stated that the cocking handle should be pulled back, it is intended that the handle should be pulled back till the sear and bent engage.

TEMPORARY STOPPAGES, GUN, LEWIS ·303-IN.

In every case of stoppage the immediate action to be taken is : (1) Ascertain that there are still cartridges in the magazine by endeavouring to rotate it. (2) If the magazine will not rotate draw back the cocking handle to its full extent, using the wood handle if necessary, and continue firing. Should this remedy fail, the cause must be looked for among the faults specified below :—

I. Position of Cocking Handle.	II. Remedy.	III. Probable Cause.	IV. Prevention of Recurrence.	V. Method of Preparation for Instructional Purposes.
I. **A.** In fired position, not having moved back though pressure on the trigger has been maintained.	(i) If the magazine can be rotated freely in the feeding direction it is empty and must be replaced.	(i) No cartridge in the chamber.		(i) Place an empty magazine on gun, pull back the cocking handle and press the trigger.
	(ii) If the magazine cannot be rotated as in (i), allow a short interval to elapse, then pull the cocking handle back and continue firing.	(ii) (a) No cartridge in the chamber, owing either to an empty space in the magazine or to a fault in feed due to insufficient rotation of the magazine. (b) Miss fire due to defective ammunition.	(ii) (a) If a succession of stoppages occur, due apparently to faults in feed, examine the magazine to see that the rim is not broken or distorted. If it is correct, examine the gun for a short or broken feed arm pawl, a broken feed arm pawl spring or stop pawls spring.	(ii) (a) For range purposes. — Leave an empty space in the magazine. (b) For range purposes. — Place a dummy cartridge in the magazine.
	(iii) If the cocking handle will not move, insert the wood handle which is carried in the spare	(iii) (a) Hard extraction, due to abnormal expansion of the cartridge case or to	Clean chamber.	(iii) Remove the magazine. Pull back the cocking handle, place a slightly damaged

TEMPORARY STOPPAGES, GUN, LEWIS, ·303-IN.—*continued.*

I—*continued.*

I.	II.	III.	IV.	V.
Position of Cocking Handle.	Remedy.	Probable Cause.	Prevention of Recurrence.	Method of Preparation for Instructional Purposes.
	parts case into the lightening hole in the cocking handle, and pull the latter back sharply. See that the empty case is ejected. Then remove the wood handle and continue firing.	dirt or rust in the chamber. (b) Fouling in gas cylinder and on head of piston, causing the latter to stick.	Clean piston and gas cylinder.	dummy cartridge in the chamber and press the trigger.
B. In fired position, having moved back and come forward	(i) If the immediate action for A (ii) fails, weigh the return spring with the spring balance. If it is light increase its weight. If it is broken exchange it. If the spring is correct, examine the striker and, if it is damaged or broken, exchange the piston rod. *Note.*—A broken return spring can usually be detected by observing the tension screw, the T-head of which will project from the pinion casing if the spring is broken. (ii) If on pulling back the cocking handle it is seen that the feed arm and magazine do not move, replace the piston rod.	(i) (a) Non-ignition of the cartridge, due to weak or broken return spring. (b) Damaged or broken striker. (ii) Broken striker post.		(i) (a) *For range purposes.* — Reduce the weight of the return spring till it has not sufficient strength to ignite the cap.
II. Back less than the length of a cartridge.	(i) Pull back the cocking handle sharply, using the wood handle if necessary. Examine the cartridge which is ejected to see if it is damaged or if the front portion of a separated case is adhering to it.	(i) (a) Owing to its being damaged the cartridge has not been able to enter the chamber completely.		(i) (a) Place a damaged dummy cartridge in the magazine. Assemble the latter to the gun; pull back the cocking handle and ease it forward gently. *For range purposes.*—Place a damaged dummy cartridge in the magazine.
		(b) Owing to the case of the previous cartridge having separated and the front portion remaining in the chamber, the cartridge cannot enter the	(i) (b) If further separations occur, change the bolt. The distance of the face of the bolt from the rear face of the barrel must be	(b) Pull back the cocking handle, place the front portion of a cartridge case which has separated near the shoulder in the chamber and press the trigger. *For range pur-*

TEMPORARY STOPPAGES, GUN, LEWIS, ·303-IN.—*continued.*

II—*continued.*

I.	II.	III.	IV.	V.
Position of Cocking Handle.	Remedy.	Probable Cause.	Prevention of Recurrence.	Method of Preparation for Instructional Purposes.
		chamber completely	tested by an armourer at the earliest opportunity.	*poses.*—File a shallow groove round a cartridge case rather more than an inch from the base and place it in the magazine. Care must be taken not to file this groove too deeply or there will be a danger of the bullet being left in the bore or of the case being separated before it reaches the chamber.
	(ii) If the cartridge is not damaged and has no portion of another case adhering to it take the clearing plug from the spare parts case, see that its centre pin is fully back, and insert the split portion into the chamber through the ejection opening. Ease the cocking handle forward so as to push the pin well forward and, keeping a firm pressure on the cocking handle, rock the handle of the plug up and down. Pull back the cocking handle, raise the safety catch, and lever back the handle of the plug and remove it from the chamber, seeing that a portion of a case is adhering to it. Knock the centre pin back and remove the separated case.	As in (i) (b).	As in (i) (b).	(l) As for (i) (b), but the case should have separated near the base, and the cocking handle must be eased gently forward. *For range purposes.*—As for (i) (b), but the groove should be near the base of the case.
III. Back about 5 inches (the bolt being back the length of a cartridge).	III. On examining the ejection opening the cartridge will be found with its bullet pressed against the base of a case which still remains in the chamber. Pull back the cocking handle and *raise the safety*	The cartridge is unable to enter the chamber, the case of the previous cartridge not having been extacted. (a) If the rim of the case is		With the cocking handle back place an empty cartridge case in the chamber and press the trigger. *For range purposes.*—As above. In remedying the stoppage *strict*

TEMPORARY STOPPAGES, GUN, LEWIS, ·303-IN.—*continued.*

I.	II.	III.	IV.	V.
Position of Cocking Handle.	Remedy.	Probable Cause.	Prevention of Recurrence.	Method of Preparation for Instructional Purposes.
III—*continued.*	*catch.* Remove the magazine and, with the cleaning rod, tap the case out of the chamber and remove it through the ejection opening.* Examine the rim of the case to see if the extractors have cut through it. Then, *seeing that the front is clear,* depress the safety catch and ease forward very gently the cocking handle to place in the chamber the cartridge which has remained under the cartridge guide spring. Draw back the cocking handle to eject this cartridge. If the rim of the case is marked by neither extractor, or by one extractor only, remove the bolt and replace the defective extractor. Then press the trigger, load and continue firing. *Note.*—The cartridge thus removed must be carefully examined to see that the bullet has not been forced into the case, in which event it would give a dangerously high pressure on firing and must be put aside.	marked by both extractors the stoppage is due to the case sticking very tightly in the chamber. (b) If the rim is not marked, or is marked by one extractor only, the stoppage is due to the failure of one or both of the extractors.		*attention must be paid to the parts in italics, and to the Not, in the column " Immediate Action."*
A. about 3 inches having back.	IV. Between 3 and 5 back, not gone fully	Pull the cocking handle back and continue firing. If found necessary the gas regulator should be turned to bring the large hole to the rear.	Though the empty case has been ejected, the bolt has not gone back far enough to engage behind the rim of the cartridge under the cartridge guide spring. This may be due to (a) Hard extraction. (b) Friction in the gas cylinder	(b) If the stoppage re-	

* The case can be removed from chamber with the modified clearing plug (No 2).

Temporary Stoppages, Gun, Lewis, ·303-in.—continued.

IV—continued.

I.	II.	III.	IV.	V.
Position of Cocking Handle.	Remedy.	Probable Cause.	Prevention of Recurrence.	Method of preparation for instructional purposes.
B. Between about 3 and 5 inches back, having gone fully back and partially forward.	(i) As in IV A. If in drawing back the cocking handle it is noticed that the resistance is slight, exchange the return spring. (ii) As in IV A. If on pressing the trigger the cocking handle only goes partially forward, draw back the cocking handle *raise the safety catch* and remove the magazine. The cartridge under the cartridge guide spring will be found to have been forced partly forward and to be resting against an empty case in the body. With the small screwdriver press back the cartridge and remove the empty case through the ejection opening. Then depress the safety catch and, *seeing that the front is clear*, ease forward the cocking handle to place the cartridge in chamber. Draw back the cocking handle to eject it, press the trigger, load, and continue firing. *Note.*— The note under III applies to this case also.	or moving part of the gun. (i) Owing to weakness or breakage of the return spring the bolt has not sufficient energy to carry the cartridge forward. (ii) Owing to a failure to eject the empty case the succeeding cartridge is carried forward against it and cannot enter the chamber. *Note.*—A broken return spring is also likely to produce stoppages with the cocking handle in other positions.	curs, clean the gas cylinder and the head of the piston. Examine the working faces of the striker post and of the cam slot in the bolt, and if they are rough change the piston rod or bolt as required. Oil all working parts. (ii) If the stoppage recurs examine the extractors and ejector and exchange any of them that may be damaged or broken.	(ii) With the cocking handle back place an empty case in the body through the ejection opening and press the trigger. *For range purposes* —As above. In remedying the stoppage *strict attention must be paid to the parts in italics and to the Note*, in the column "Immediate Action."

TEMPORARY STOPPAGES, GUN, LEWIS, ·303-IN.—*continued.*

IV.—*continued.*

I.	II.	III.	IV.	V.
Position of Cocking Handle.	Remedy.	Probable Cause.	Prevention of Recurrence.	Method of Preparation for Instructional Purposes.
	(iii) If the cocking handle cannot be moved easily, remove the magazine, when it will be seen that the bullet of the cartridge under the cartridge guide spring has dipped and that the bolt has therefore missed the rim and caught on the body of the cartridge case, while the feed arm has moved partly over the cartridge and is holding it down. Pull back the cocking handle, if necessary using the wood handle, replace the magazine and continue firing.	(iii) Fault in feed.	(iii) If the stoppage recurs, examine the cartridge guide spring and if it is weak or broken replace it.	(iii) Remove the magazine, place a dummy cartridge on the feed arm, and draw back the cocking handle. Force the bullet end of the cartridge down slightly with the screwdriver and press the trigger.
V. More than 5 inches back.	(i) Remove the magazine, when it will be seen that the point of the bullet has caught against the front end of the cartridge opening in the body or the feed arm. Pull back the cocking handle and, if the jar does not make the point of the bullet drop, force it down till it is clear. Replace the magazine and continue firing.	(i) Fault in feed due to (a) The piston having been driven back with too much violence and the sharp rebound not having given the cartridge guide spring time to act properly. (b) Weak or broken cartridge guide spring.	(i) (a) I the large hole o the gas regulator is to the rear, turn the regulator so as to bring the small hole into operation. Increase the weight of the return spring if necessary. (b) Replace the spring.	
	(ii) If the cocking handle cannot be pulled back, remove the magazine. The cocking handle will then fly forward, and a cartridge will be found on the feed arm.	(ii) Fault in feed due to a broken magazine rim. The pressure of the pawl on the broken part will force it forward and jam the cartridge so that it cannot leave the magazine till the latter is relieved from the pressure, when the cartridge will fall out on to the feed arm.		(ii) Use a broken magazine if one is available. *For range purposes.*—As above.
	(iii) If on removing the magazine as in	(iii) Fault in feed due to a		(iii) No attempt must be made to

TEMPORARY STOPPAGES, GUN, LEWIS, ·303-IN.—*continued.*

I.	II.	III.	IV.	V.
Position of Cocking Handle.	Remedy.	Probable Cause.	Prevention of Recurrence.	Method of Preparation for Instructional Purposes.
V—*continued.*	(ii) It is found that a cartridge is jammed under the tongue on the body cover, it may be possible to force the cartridge clear of the tongue with the small screwdriver. If not, remove the butt or spade handle grip, slide the trigger guard slightly back, and remove the body cover, when the cartridge can be removed. In all cases replace the cartridge guide spring.	wrongly assembled or broken cartridge guide spring. If the spring is wrongly assembled the probability is that it will be broken by the first cartridge which is forced under it.		reproduce this stoppage for either instructional or range purposes.

Note.—If, when the trigger is released, the gun does not stop firing it indicates either that the sear cannot rise owing to damage to the mechanism contained in the trigger guard, or that the sear or bent are damaged or broken. It is not possible to stop the gun till the cartridges in the magazine are expended. When the gun stops the bent on the piston rod and the trigger mechanism must be examined and any necessary replacements made.

GUN, HOTCHKISS, ·303-in.
(Approved May, 1917, L. of C., para. 18419.)
GENERAL DESCRIPTION.

Weight of gun	about 28 lbs.
Length overall	36 inches.
Length of barrel	23¼ ,,
Length of feed strips	16½ ,, .
Length of actuator spring	13 ,,
Rifling	Enfield; 5 grooves; 1 turn in ten inches.
Ammunition	·303-in., Mark. VII.

The gun comprises a single barrel, receiver, guard and stock rigidly assembled. Guided in the receiver parallel to and below the barrel is the piston which by its reciprocating motion assures the automatic action of the gun. This reciprocating motion is brought about as follows: When the bullet in its passage through the bore has passed a port connecting the bore with the gas nozzle, a small portion of the powder gas issues from the nozzle and, impinging in the cup-shaped forward extremity of the piston, throws it to the rear. The actuator spring compressed by the piston in its rearward movement now returns the piston to its initial position.

In its movement to the rear the piston, which is accompanied by the breech block, opens the breech, extracts and ejects the spent cartridge case, and brings a fresh cartridge to the loading position. In its forward movement a cartridge is pushed into the chamber, the breech locked, and the shot fired.

The cartridges are fed into the gun on flat, tempered steel strips of 30 rounds each.

A folding barrel rest is provided for steadying the barrel when firing in the phone position which will ordinarily be taken.

For aircraft the gun is mounted on a crutch, and the stock may be replaced by a pistol grip.

The operation of the gun requires but one man, who loads and fires. If a second operator loads, the speed of fire is increased from 250 to 400 rounds per minute.

Nomenclature of Parts of Gun.

Barrel	With trunnion ring; gas nozzle ring; orifice screw; gas cylinder support; fore sight carrier; fore sight.*
Regulator	
Receiver	With bottom plate; front feed guide; rear feed guide; cartridge base stop; feed piece cover; closing spring; rear sight base; rear sight screw.

---

* Foresights marked "H," "M," "L," "LL" are provided and these should correspond with similar marks on the foresight carrier. "H" mean height; "M" medium; "L" low; "LL" very low.

Hand guard ... With catches for legs; catch springs.
Locking nut.
Locking screw.
Cocking handle.
Guard with stock. With actuator spring seat; hinged strap; elevating screw tube; elevating screw slide; slide spring,
Barrel rest.
Elevating mechanism ... With outer screw; inner screw; base.

Working Parts:—

Piston.	Sear.
Fermeture nut.	Trigger.
Breech block.	Feed piece.
Extractor.	Feed spring.
Firing pin.	Recoil spring.
Ejector.	Ejector spring.
Ejector cap.	Sear spring.
Cartridge stop.	Cartridge stop spring.
Cartridge stop holder.	Extractor spring.

To Strip and Assemble the Gun.

1st.—*Close the breech.*
   (a) Lift the feed piece to its highest position by pressing up on its lower end as for loading. This releases the shoulder of the piston from the feed piece and allows it to move forward slightly and rest on the sear.
   (b) Pull the trigger, the cocking handle being set at "R" or "A." As this releases the sear, the piston is propelled forward by the actuator spring and the breech closed as when firing.

2nd.—*Remove the cocking handle.*
   (a) Throw the cocking handle knob to the left slightly past the vertical and against the stop.
   (b) Draw the cocking handle back about $\frac{1}{2}$ in. and then throw the knob to the right as far as possible to an angle of about 45°. By this movement the cocking handle is released from the piston.
   (c) Withdraw the cocking handle to the rear.

3rd.—*Remove the guard.*
   (a) Unscrew the locking screw on the left side of the receiver three turns.
   (b) Grasp the receiver firmly with the left hand and the stock or pistol grip with the right. Push the stock forward about $\frac{3}{8}$ in. and then bring it straight down, separating it from the receiver. This combined movement will be learned after a few trials.
   The firing gear (sear, sear spring, and trigger) remains with the guard.

4th.—*Withdraw the recoil spring from the receiver.*

5th.—*Remove the recoiling mechanism.*
  (a) Insert the cocking handle in the piston and push it forward as far as it will go, the knob inclined at about 45° to the right. When home, turn the knob to the vertical position so as to engage the lugs at the forward end with the piston.
  (b) Draw the cocking handle to the rear, and with it the piston, breech block, extractor, and firing pin.

6th.—*Remove the feed spring.*
  (a) Disengage the feed spring from the button at the top of the feed piece, springing it up with the fore-finger of the right hand by means of the hooked portion projecting to the rear.
  (b) Dismount the feed spring by pushing it to the rear with the left hand by means of the knurled button, at the same time springing it up sufficiently with the right hand to clear the pawl from the rear feed guide.

7th.—*Remove the feed piece.*
  (a) Throw open the feed piece cover by means of the knurled knob.
  (b) Lift leaf of rear sight.
  (c) Lift the feed piece to its highest position and turn through an angle of 180° so that the lever points to the rear. As the flattened portion of the axis is now opposite the corresponding slot in the upper bearing, the feed piece may be removed to the rear.

8th.—*Remove the ejector.*
  (a) By means of the key unscrew the ejector cap and remove it.
  (b) Lift out the ejector spring and then the ejector.

9th.—*Remove the barrel.*
  (a) Unscrew the barrel locking nut $\frac{1}{6}$th of a turn to a stop with the right hand, using the dismounting wrench.
  (b) Remove the barrel by drawing it straight to the front.

10th.—*Remove the hand guard.*
  (a) Turn the locking nut to the left sufficiently to free its stud from engagement with the hand guard. (This stud serves to hold the hand guard in place while the barrel is being mounted or dismounted.)
  (b) Remove the hand guard by drawing it to the front.

11th.—*Unscrew and remove the locking nut.*

12th.—*Remove the fermeture nut.*

13th.—*Remove the firing pin.*

Reverse the breech block, and the firing pin will fall into the hand.

14th.—*Remove the extractor.*
  (*a*) Grasp the breech block with the left hand, and the hand extractor with the right; insert the hook portion of the latter between the last and before last coil of the extractor spring, compress the spring, tilt the end out of its seat, and remove it.
  (*b*) By holding the breech block upwards, the extractor will fall out.

15th.—*Remove the firing gear from the guard.*
  (*a*) Hold the stock between the knees, the guard to the front.
  (*b*) With the right hand lift the hooked arm of the trigger sufficiently to clear it entirely from the vertical lever of the sear.
  (*c*) With the left hand catch the knurled button forming the outer extremity of the sear axis and draw to the left sufficiently to free the right hand end of the axis from its pocket. Now lift the sear vertically from the guard.
  (*d*) Lift the trigger upward and forward, separating it and the sear with spring attached from the guard.
  (*e*) Detach the respective ends of the spring from the sear and trigger.

16th.—*Remove the cartridge stop.*
  (*a*) Unscrew the cartridge stop holder by means of the dismounting wrench.
  (*b*) Withdraw the cartridge stop spring and the cartridge stop.

Assembling.

1st—*Mount in order the following parts*: Fermeture nut, locking nut, hand guard, barrel, ejector, spring and cap, feed piece and spring.

2nd.—*Assemble* the trigger, sear, and sear spring, and then mount them in guard.

3rd.—*Mount the recoiling parts in the receiver.*
  (*a*) Assemble the extractor with the breech block.
  (*b*) Mount the firing pin, bringing it to its rearmost position and turning the head to the left behind the shoulder in the breech block.
  (*c*) Engage the piston tang in the under slot of the breech block. (The rear face of the tang should abut against the rear wall of the slot, and the under tang of the firing

pin should engage in the corresponding groove in the piston tang.)

(d) Turn the fermeture nut to the open position by passing the first finger of the left hand in the ejection slot of the receiver. (When in the open position the ejection slot in the fermeture nut coincides with the ejection slot in the receiver.)

(e) With the right hand grasp the rear of the piston assembled with the breech block as per (c), placing the thumb on the head of the firing pin so as to hold it turned to the left behind the shoulder of the breech block.

(f) Insert the piston assembled with the breech block in the rear of the receiver and push it forward with the right hand until it comes to a stop. (Its rear face will now be about $1\frac{1}{2}$ in. forward of the rear of the receiver.'

N.B.—It is imperative that the head of the firing pin be turned completely to the left, and that the fermeture nut be at the open position. See (d) and (e.) The mechanism should slip into place easily, forcing being neither necessary nor permissible.

(g) While pressing on the lower end of the feed piece with the right hand so as to bring it to its highest position, push forward the piston with the left hand until the breech is closed.

4th—*Insert the recoil spring* in the piston and push forward, allowing a few inches to project to the rear of the receiver.

5th—*Mount the guard.*

(a) Grasp the pistol grip with the right hand as for firing, making sure that the firing gear is properly mounted by pulling the trigger several times.

(b) Engage the projecting end of the recoil spring in its seat in the guard.

(c) Bring the guard to a position under the receiver such that the two lugs on its head are opposite their mortises in the rear of the receiver, the trunnions at the front being below and slightly in advance of their sockets in the bottom of the receiver. In order that the end of the actuator spring remain engaged to its seat in the guard, it may be held in place by means of the end of the cocking handle shank.

(d) Engage the lugs in their mortises and the trunnions in their sockets by raising the guard vertically.

(e) Draw the guard to the rear until solidly seated in the receiver

(f) Screw up the locking screw.

6th—*Mount the cocking handle.*
- (a) Insert the shank of the cocking handle in the opening in the guard, the knob inclined at 45° to the right, and push forward to a stop.
- (b) Throw the knob to the left to a stop.
- (c) Push the cocking handle forward until home, and then throw the knob to the right and down as far as it will go.

In order to replace a defective extractor or firing pin, proceed as follows:
- 1st.—Close the breech.
- 2nd.—Remove the cocking handle.
- 3rd.—Remove the guard.
- 4th.—Withdraw the recoil spring.
- 5th.—Remove the recoiling mechanism.

Replace the defective part by a spare, and mount by reversing the operations.

The extractor and extractor spring can also be removed without stripping the gun, as follows:
- 1st.—Insert an empty cartridge case in the ejection slot, perpendicular to the chamber.
- 2nd.—Close the breech gently, *i.e.*, by holding it back with the cocking handle, on to the empty cartridge case, thus giving access to the extractor and extractor spring.
- 3rd.—Remove the extractor spring and extractor by means of the hand extractor.

Replace the defective part by a spare, cock the gun, and withdraw the empty cartridge case.

USE OF THE REGULATOR.

In order that the working of the gun may be regular, sufficient power must be available to ensure complete recoil of the piston. The amount of power necessary may vary because of insufficient oiling, dust, or fouling in the mechanism, etc. Then, again, the pressure of the powder gases may vary because of the temperature, deteriorated powder, or badly-worn rifling.

The regulator affords means of varying the power which works the gun. Under normal conditions it should be set at 25.

To test the automatic action, fire several shots with the regulator set at 25 and the cocking handle at R, and observe:

- (a) *One shot should be fired at each pull of the trigger.*
    If more than one shot is fired at a time, it shows that the piston does not recoil sufficiently after each shot to catch on the sear.
- (b) *The claw of the pawl should catch in the opening in the strip at each shot.* If the pawl rides on top of the strip

instead of catching, it shows that the piston does not recoil sufficiently to throw the feed lever through a complete stroke.

(c) *The ejection should be regular and energetic.*

If these three points are not satisfactory it may be concluded that there is a lack of power, and the regulator should be screwed up from 5 to 10 divisions.

ACTION OF THE MECHANISM.

In order to load, the breech must be opened by means of the cocking handle. As the piston is drawn back, cams on its upper face turn the fermeture nut a partial revolution, disengaging its interrupted threads from corresponding threads on the nose of breech block. This unlocks the breech. Under the action of its spring, the feed piece engages with a shoulder on the piston and locks it in its rearmost position.

To permit the introduction of the feed strip, the feed piece must be lifted to its highest position by pressing up on its lower end. This frees it from the shoulder of the piston, which latter moves forward slightly under the action of its spring and engages with the sear. The feed strip may now be introduced into the guides, cartridge side down, and should be pushed forward until the pawl forming part of the feed spring engages with it, so as to prevent any backward movement.

When the trigger is pulled, the piston, accompanied by the breech block, is propelled forward by the recoil spring; the breech block pushes a cartridge from the feed strip into the chamber; the cams on the upper face of the piston act on the fermeture nut locking the breech; the firing pin is driven against the cap and the shot fired.

When the bullet in its passage through the bore has passed the port leading to the gas nozzle, a small portion of the powder gas, conducted by the port and the gas nozzle, impinges in the cup-shaped forward extremity of the piston, and drives it to the rear. As already explained, the breech is now unlocked by the action of the piston cams on the fermeture nut, the breech block is withdrawn, along with the extractor holding the spent cartridge case, which latter, when entirely extracted, is ejected when its head strikes the ejector.

Towards the end of the backward stroke of the piston, a cam on its side imparts a slight rotary movement to the feed piece, which advances the feed strip sufficiently to bring the following cartridge to the loading position.

Its last cartridge having been fired, the exhausted strip is ejected from the gun. Under the action of its spring, the feed piece, which has been held up by the strip, now descends and, engaging with the shoulder of the piston, locks the breech open.

All is now ready for the introduction of another strip. Feed piece must again be lifted.

The firing gear may be set for continuous firing, single shots, or safety, by turning the cocking handle to the positions marked "A," "R," and "S" respectively.

When set at "A" (automatic), so long as the trigger is held back the piston is free to move forward again under the action of the actuator spring. As a result, the gun fires continuously until the strip is exhausted or the trigger released.

When set at "R" (repetition), a separate pull of the trigger is required for each shot, as the sear engages with the piston each time the latter recoils, thus stopping the firing.

When set at "S" (safety), the trigger is locked, and cannot be pulled back so as to release the sear from the piston. As a result the gun cannot be fired.

ACCIDENTAL STOPPAGES IN THE AUTOMATIC ACTION OF THE GUN.

In case of a jam always proceed as follows:—

(a) Open the breech completely by means of the cocking handle.

(b) Remove the jammed cartridge through the ejection slot by using the hand ejector or cleaning rod as the case may be, and see that the chamber is clear.

(c) Withdraw the strip if some remedy is to be applied. Otherwise push it forward, bringing the next cartridge to the loading position.

STOPPAGES AND THEIR REMEDIES.

(1) *Jam on the first round of a strip.*

The strip was probably not pushed completely home before the trigger was pulled. Always push forward the strip until the pawl catches, so that both strip and cartridge are positively held in the loading position.

(2) *Missfire.*

Eject the defective cartridge by cocking the gun, and continue firing.

N.B.—A loose cap falling into the mechanism may cause repeated missfires. Dismount the piston and breech block so as to remove the cap, which will usually be found either in the piston cams or in the fermeture nut near the entrance to the chamber.

Missfires may also be due to a weakened recoil spring. In this case replace the spring with the spare.

(3) *Bad introduction.*

The cartridge jams at the entrance to the chamber when being pushed forward by the breech block. The bullet of the cartridge in question may have been imperfectly seated due to defective crimping or the cartridge insufficiently held by the clips of the feed strip.

In the latter case the strip should be laid aside for re-sizing.

Another cause of bad introductions is incomplete feeding forward of the strip, due to lack of power. In this case screw up the regulator 5 to 10 divisions.

(4) *Incomplete ejection of the spent cartridge case.*

This is due to lack of power. Screw up the regulator 5 to 10 divisions.

CONDEMNATION OF MACHINE GUN BARRELS.

As far as the *Land Service* is concerned, machine-gun barrels will, in future, be condemned as unserviceable if they fail to reach the standard of accuracy detailed in Equipment Regulations (see para. 212, E.R., Part I., 1912, Section VI.), condemnation by gauging being abolished.

The sentencing of unserviceable barrels D.P. will be done by the Chief Inspector of Small Arms, Enfield Lock, as hitherto.

For *Naval Service* the following is the procedure for condemnation of barrels:—

(1) Barrel cleaned and free from metallic fouling, &c., as with rifles and carbines. The ·303-in. plug should run.
(2) The coppering on exterior at muzzle and breech end not to be chipped or blistered.
(3) The ·307-in. plug enters $\frac{1}{4}$ inch at muzzle.
(4) The ·309-in. ,, ,, 1 inch at breech.
 (*i.e.*, to line engraved on rods, plug.)
(5) The No. 1 lead plug enters the breech $\frac{7}{16}$ inch.

GENERAL INSTRUCTIONS FOR THE MAINTENANCE AND PRESERVATION OF GUNS.

The manner in which machine guns are dealt with as equipment in the Land Service is laid down in Equipment Regulations as under :—

    Regular Army, Parts 1 and 2.
    Special Reserve, Part 1, and Section XVI., Part 2.
    Territorial Force, Part 3.

Guns are issued with the bright gunmetal parts painted Service colour. It is, however, at the discretion of General Officers Commanding, in the case of armament guns, to vary this colour to suit local requirements.

For cleaning and oiling machine guns and mountings in the hands of troops, the following stores are allowed per annum in peace for one gun and its mounting :—

Flannelette, Mark III	11 yards.
Old linen	3 lbs.
Mineral oil, burning	$\frac{1}{2}$ pint.
Oil, lubricating, G.S.	8 pints.
Spirits of turpentine	1 pint.
Dubbing	$\frac{1}{2}$ lb.
Soap, yellow	4 bars.

When guns are returned to store, packed for transmission, or stowed away in any place where they cannot be readily examined, the barrels and unpainted parts should be coated with "Composition, preserving arms." The mixture is to be made hot, and a piece of flannel dipped in it with which the exterior parts will be dabbed. To coat the inside of the barrels draw a bunch of lamp cotton, well saturated with the mixture, through from both ends; the lamp cotton is to be attached to a piece of twisted copper wire.

In the case of Vickers and Maxim guns, in frosty weather, when water is kept in the barrel casing, a blanket or some other thick covering should be kept wrapped round the barrel casing to prevent the water freezing. The working parts of the gun should only be slightly oiled with a lightly-oiled rag. In climates where the temperature is likely to fall much below freezing point, not more than about five pints of water should be put into the barrel casing (50 per cent. of glycerine, or 33 per cent. of glycerine residue, mixed with the water will prevent it from freezing quickly).

History sheet.—A memorandum of examination or history sheet accompanies each gun when issued in peace time. It will be carefully preserved and will be handed over with the gun to which it belongs whenever the gun is transferred from the charge of one officer to that of another, particulars being duly recorded. An immediate record will be made in the sheets of any accident which may happen to the gun, and of the result of each official examination it may undergo. On every occasion on which ball ammunition is fired, the number of rounds fired will be shown, the number of the barrel being inserted in the column of remarks.

Barrels.—A new, or part worn but serviceable, barrel is issued as a part of each gun. This barrel is only to be used for firing ball ammunition.

An old barrel, marked D.P., is also issued, to be used only for drill purposes. A second old barrel, marked D.P.B., is issued, to be used only for firing blank ammunition. On mobilization these three barrels are to be returned to store. In addition, two new barrels (armament, one) are issued with each gun and are to be kept in store and only taken into use on mobilization, one in the gun and one spare. New barrels in store are distinguished by a band of white paint round the centre.

www.ingramcontent.com/pod-product-compliance
Lightning Source LLC
Chambersburg PA
CBHW060201050426
42446CB00013B/2938

belongs whenever the gun is transferred from the charge of one officer to that of another, particulars being duly recorded. An immediate record will be made in the sheets of any accident which may happen to the gun, and of the result of each official examination it may undergo. On every occasion on which ball ammunition is fired, the number of rounds fired will be shown, the number of the barrel being inserted in the column of remarks.

Barrels.—A new, or part worn but serviceable, barrel is issued as a part of each gun. This barrel is only to be used for firing ball ammunition.

An old barrel, marked D.P., is also issued, to be used only for drill purposes. A second old barrel, marked D.P.B., is issued, to be used only for firing blank ammunition. On mobilization these three barrels are to be returned to store. In addition, two new barrels (armament, one) are issued with each gun and are to be kept in store and only taken into use on mobilization, one in the gun and one spare. New barrels in store are distinguished by a band of white paint round the centre.

www.ingramcontent.com/pod-product-compliance
Lightning Source LLC
Chambersburg PA
CBHW060201050426
42446CB00013B/2938